Black Threatening Invisible: My Journey In Corporate America

Black Threatening Invisible: My Journey In Corporate America

A SURVIVAL GUIDE OF SORTS

* * *

S. K. Chapman

Printed in the United States of America.
ISBN: 0692783024
ISBN-13: 9780692783023
Library of Congress Control Number: 2016915837
MB Books, Elkhorn, NE

www.blackthreateninginvisible.com.
blackthreateninginvisible@gmail.com.

Contents

Dedication

To my dear son, Morgan: Your mom and I have only known you for twenty months, but during that time, you've changed us in ways we never imagined and at a pace that continues to astound us. Because of you, we are better people and better spouses, and every day we strive to be better parents to such a deserving little boy. We assumed we'd be teaching you, but you continue to teach us the real meaning of patience, understanding, and unconditional love. Your presence serves as a reminder of the preciousness of life and of the importance of enjoying the small things, such as when you first said "Da-Da" or took your first step. You were slow to take your first step, which we now know is fitting for your personality. Everything is on your time.

Our love for you is immeasurable, and we're thankful to God for the gift of bringing you into this world. It's your mom's and my prayer that each day of your life will be more fulfilling and rewarding than the last. Fatherhood is a privilege and not a right, and it's an honor to have the privilege to be your father. While I'll surely make many mistakes along the way, I pray that you'll charge those mistakes to my head and not my heart, since I would never intentionally harm you.

Two weeks after your birth, while you were sleeping peacefully in your crib, with suffocating guilt and a heavy heart, I whispered these two words in your ear: "I'm sorry."

* I was sorry because I brought you into a world that will treat black people, even black babies, with contempt and suspicion.
* I was sorry because the mere color of your skin will intimidate, frighten, and cause discomfort to others.
* I was sorry because the thought of innocent black babies like yourself once being used as alligator bait during the Jim Crow era infuriates me.
* I was sorry because society will never see you the way your mom and I see you. Society will often fail to see you at all, and that's a sad truth.
* I was sorry because I brought you into a world where your skin color may one day cost you your life.

It's common for me to become lost staring into those big, bright eyes of yours, filled with promise, hope, and innocence. Sometimes you stare back at me with an intensity and focus unbefitting a baby, and I can't help but wonder what you must be thinking. I'm comforted by the belief that your thoughts are pure and innocent. I wish I could say the same of my own thoughts.

Thoughts of your future frighten me and have filled me with anxiety since the day your mom and I, with great care, drove you home from the hospital on that cold and rainy Tuesday morning. I'm consumed by thoughts of how your skin color will affect the rest of your life. A more unbearable thought is if the color of your skin will one day cost you your life.

Though your mom and I have the best intentions of raising a son with integrity, morals, and strong character, we can't change your skin color, nor would we want to. That doesn't stop us from worrying about your future. Living life as black people hasn't been easy for us and won't be easy for you. Morgan, my son, I dedicate this book to you.

Acknowledgments

* * *

Special thanks to my wife for being an amazing mother, gifted physician, and an all-around remarkable person. You have given me the greatest gift life has to offer: our adorable son.

I couldn't have written this book without your understanding: for the many nights you went to bed alone because my promise to join you after I'd completed "just one more paragraph" resulted in you not seeing me until the next morning; for the many nights when the glow of my nightlight or the noise from the keyboard made it difficult for you to fall asleep; for the many nights you arose from bed to persuade me to start fresh tomorrow because I'd fallen asleep while working on this book.

I couldn't have written this book without your unwavering support. When I wanted to quit, you encouraged me to keep going. When I wanted to take a break, you reminded me of the saying "tomorrow's not promised."

When I wanted to scale back on the details, you encouraged me to remain true to my experiences and to the experiences of other black professionals who've trusted me with their stories. When I proclaimed for the hundredth time that I'd completed writing the content for this book, you gave me a congratulatory high-five—even though you knew I was not.

In a world where everyone is trying to be someone else, you encourage me to be myself.

Thanks to the hundred-plus black professionals who have shared details of their professional lives with me; I hope to have captured your sentiments and made you proud.

Thanks to my mom for your gifts of life, strength, and perseverance. You are the strongest woman I know and the reason I do not shrink in the face of adversity.

Thanks to my mentor, Dr. Bailey, for showing me that association does not always breed assimilation.

Thanks to my best friend, Lovell. I could search the world several times over and never find another who is half the friend you are. Did you ever think our chance meeting in college would result in a lifelong friendship?

Thanks to my cousin Claxton for the many challenging and thought-provoking conversations we've had over the years. Thanks to you, I know a thousand more aphorisms than any one person should know.

Thanks to my siblings for your perspective and grounding.

Thanks to my in-laws for always counterbalancing my thoughts with the Word of God, especially Psalm 31.

Thanks to my brother-in-law and sister-in-law for your endless support throughout the book-writing process.

Many thanks to the editing, marketing, publishing, and legal teams, and to the book designer and photographer, for your collective expertise and support.

A special thanks to all those who have filled my path with obstacles over the years. It is because of you I am so resilient today.

Preface: A Phone Conversation

* * *

MOTIVATION CAN SOMETIMES COME FROM where you least expect it. Who knew a conversation with a close friend one morning during a thirty-minute commute to work would set me on a path to writing my first literary piece so that I could share the frustrations and challenges I and many other black professionals regularly encounter in corporate America.

Although my friend and I are close in age, I've always thought of him as my younger and more ambitious brother. While I and other college students focused on pretty girls and thought little about our plans following college, he had a much broader focus. He focused on becoming the CEO of his own IT company. His insensibility to his skin color made me focus on finding drug-free acquaintances. He was obviously under the influence of something reality altering if he thought this was even remotely possible. I dared not question this aloud though.

As a small-minded kid from humble beginnings, I struggled to dream beyond my immediate surroundings and self-perceived limitations. I remember occasionally tagging along with my mom to clean the houses of wealthy families who lived on the "other side of the tracks". I was awestruck by the sight of these homes that had seemingly hundreds of windows and driveways that extended for miles. Family photos lining the fireplace mantel and stairwell walls left no room to question. These families were happy and they weren't black. While following my mom around from one large room to the next, I'd tell myself that someday I'd own the same even though I didn't believe a word of it.

I grew up believing that having plans for after high school was for the kids who lived in those big houses on the other side of the tracks. I didn't need any planning for what I'd be doing after high school. The natural progression for someone like me was to land one of the local factory jobs (there were plenty at one time), buy designer wheels and an eardrum-bursting stereo for my Honda Accord, and at some point move into my own apartment. What could derail a well-considered and foolproof plan like that? As the saying goes, if you want to make God laugh, tell Him what your plans are. God's laughter must have been thunderous, since my plans didn't work out as I had hoped. After I graduated from high school, I remember my dad, an army veteran, saying that he didn't care if I chose a four-year college, a community college, or the military. He wanted me to get off the couch, so off to college I went.

The buyer's remorse of attending college was immediate. I found the couch to be more enjoyable than the daily grind of college and having to listen to someone, I barely knew dreaming aloud about becoming a CEO—not just of *an* IT company but of *his* IT company. There was no denying that he was unlike any black person I'd ever met—which was not saying much, considering that many of my high school classmates took the same path after high school as I did. Despite our differences on realistic vs unrealistic goals, the dreamer and I had many things in common. It didn't take long for us to become inseparable friends, nor did it take long for his ambition to rub off on me. We eventually went into business managing a computer company he'd started before we met.

Although he took me on as a partner, I felt more like an apprentice. I had no experience building or servicing computers or running a business. He taught me a lot and tapped into the geek inside me that I didn't know existed. In no time at all, I knew the intricacies of motherboards, random access memory (RAM), graphic cards, advanced micro devices (AMD) and Intel processors, and the Windows and Linux operating systems, among other things. Our business objective was to lure customers away from the two conglomerate big box stores in the area. Competing in terms of price wasn't an option for us because of their ability to buy low and sell high, thus resulting in huge profit margins. Instead, we focused on their weaknesses, which made for a simple business plan. People will pay a higher price for a computer if they receive personalization options and in-house support at no additional charge. Our customer base started with students but in no time at all, grew to include university faculty, various companies, and other organizations throughout the city of Greensboro.

The profits were meager and could barely sustain our lifestyle mostly subsisting on ramen noodles and deli meat—but working for ourselves (combined with the experience I gained co-managing a business) was gratifying despite the hard work and sacrifices of juggling a full college course load with our business commitments. As if my plate weren't full enough, I also waited tables at night and mentored underserved kids in the community on the weekends.

This is a picture of our first sales flyer.

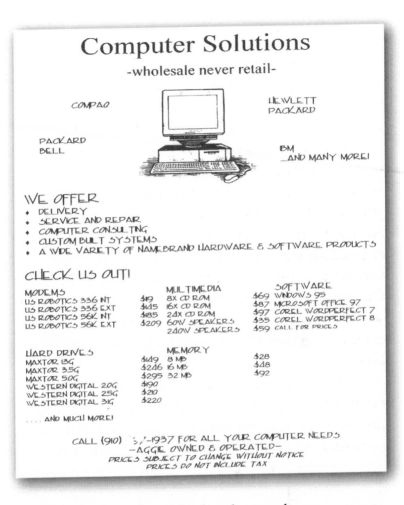

We maintained a tight bond over the next twenty years, despite the distance and the fact that we both led very busy lives. Although my friend has yet to achieve CEO status, his professional trajectory is pointing him in the right direction. After he graduated from college, he accepted a position as a software developer for a major credit-card institution. He used this technical position as a springboard to positions that were better suited to his focus area, which was business growth and development. He later landed a position working for the chief information officer (CIO) of one of the largest financial-services-holding companies in the United States. His ambition only intensified over the years. Today he's an IT process architect and a full-time student enrolled in a rigorous cross-continent MBA program. He also has an impressive real estate and stock portfolio and owns several businesses, including a soybean farm.

My path after college was not much different from his. After I graduated, I accepted a job as a software engineer for a company that specializes in the development of e-commerce and B2B (business-to-business) software. However, software engineering was not as rewarding or fast-paced a job as I had hoped, which prompted me to explore other career options. The complexity and multiple offerings of network engineering won me over, and I put down the books on JAVA and IBM's Rational Rose and picked up books on Cisco routing and switching.

I worked for a variety of telecommunication giants as a network engineer, including AT&T, UUNET, and MCI WorldCom, as well as America Online (AOL), the goliath of the early Internet era. The proto-Facebook/

Google was once the nation's largest Internet service provider, with an estimated value of $125 billion. Working at AOL during the dot-com era was wild and crazy, as you might imagine. Timing was also on my side as working for AOL during a time when stock options were more important than someone's starting salary, was also financially rewarding. I once read a statistic that AOL churned out over three thousand millionaires.[1] While I have no way to validate this statistic, I can confirm firsthand that the most important date to know as an AOL employee was the vesting dates of your stock options.

All good things must come to an end, and I sensed the end of an AOL-era was near. The increasing demand for faster and more reliable Internet bandwidth, coupled with AOL's reluctance to shift its focus from dial-up to broadband technology, started the downward spiral. To proactively choose my next professional path, I resigned from AOL and took my engineering acumen to more stable grounds—the public sector.

Still filled with the entrepreneurial spirit I'd obtained in college, I launched an IT-consulting business in which I provided various aspects of IT services and support. I started a mail-order business selling various self-written how-to guides, such as (among others) *Building a*

1   Annie Gowen, "The New Gilded Age: Rise of the Slacker Millionaires," *Washington Post*, August 1, 1999, accessed February 10, 2017, http://www.washingtonpost.com/wp-srv/style/daily/aug99/gilded1.htm.

Webpage Using HTML, *Troubleshooting Computers*, *Building Computers*, and *Starting a Business*. Besides launching several e-commerce businesses, I also started a greeting-card business called Kaboom! Cards. I invested in real estate and by the age of thirty-three, I had bought and sold five properties ranging from my first purchase for $181,000 in 2001 to a purchase price of more than $600,000 a few years later. Perhaps it pays to dream big.

Over the years, my friend and I also kept each other up to date on the latest happenings in our lives, both personally and professionally. Our discussion topics run the gamut, from life to love and all things in between. On one particular morning, one of these "in between" discussions was that my friend needed my advice on a few challenges he faced at work. He believed his boss had no interest in his professional development, yet she seemed invested in the development of his nonblack peers. He was frustrated by the years of nebulous tasks, unrealistic deadlines, lack of mentoring or support; his boss expected him to turn "chicken shit into chicken salad," as he crudely put it.

If he shared these concerns with his boss, this only confirmed her assumptions that he was in over his head; she'd then reassign the task to a nonblack peer, who'd receive dedicated personnel resources to assist and open-door access to her mentorship and guidance without condemnation—two luxuries he didn't receive.

The confidence he'd previously had while working for the CIO—who'd lauded him as an exceptional employee with natural leadership ability—was fading fast under the tutelage of his current boss.

After I listened to his all-too-familiar stories, my first order of business was to inject in him a much-needed boost of confidence by mentioning his many accomplishments to him. It was also important to remind him of one of the first life lessons that many black parents instill in their kids: blacks have to work twice as hard to receive half the recognition that our nonblack counterparts receive. As expected, he'd heard the same life lesson from his parents. What puzzled me the most about this conversation was that he'd never shared a workplace frustration or challenge with me until now. Was it possible that he was the first person to debunk my belief that all black professionals—regardless of employer, title, rank, or degrees—experience varying levels of microaggression in the workplace because of their skin color? He agreed that he seemed to be such an exception; in hindsight, however, he also said that he'd relied on excuses to justify how others treated him. He had run out of excuses.

Over the years, I've shared with him countless stories of frustration and challenges that I experienced in the workplace, so he came to the right person for advice on how to survive corporate America while black. Based on everything he'd shared with me—and I was mindful that this sharing was one-sided—I knew I could help him in a few areas. I passed along techniques for strengthening communication with his boss, workplace tools that he could use to shape and manage the expectations of his boss, and strategies he could use to anticipate the needs of his boss. I also provided constructive criticism on areas he could improve on in himself.

After thanking me for allowing him to vent and for the professional advice, he asked me a question that first ignited the fire within me to write this book: "Who will prepare our sons for their professional journey being Black, Threatening, and Invisible in corporate America?"

At the time of this writing, he is a proud and doting dad to an adorable six-year-old son, and I am a proud dad to a precocious, energetic, and independent two-year-old son. His question made me pause and think about my mortality for the first time since I'd become a dad. The phrase "tomorrow's not promised" also came to mind as I thought back to the unexpected passing of my father a little over a decade ago. My dad's Monday started like any other day. On this day, however, he would shower, shave, lace his shoes, and leave the house for the last time. My dad dropped dead a few hours after he'd arrived at work. The dreaded phone-call notification of his untimely passing has been on a recurring loop in my head ever since.

The great memories we shared bring me solace, and my faith in God, and the belief that I'll see my dad again, brings me peace.

The question my friend posed was a wake-up call that I may not be around to pass along any of the personal and professional life's lessons to my son that my dad passed along to me. At that moment, the answer to his question was obvious: I will do it. I'll write a book to share professional life's lessons with my son, my best friend's son, and, with an empathetic and heavy heart, for the anonymous "Heartbroken Mom" who wrote the following words in an online forum.

Where can I go? A friend and I were talking the other day about our boys and what it will be like when they are married and out in the workforce. I instantly became angry, not at her but at the thought that I don't get to think about those things. My mind won't let me wander into that territory. You see, my babies are brown, and hers are white. When I look at them, I don't see their future; instead, I feel guilt that I created them only to send them off into a world that will judge them based on their skin color. I cry for them inside because they have no idea what lies ahead. That sentence is enough to make me cry right now. Please take my word for it—they are just like your littles! They laugh, play games, talk back, refuse to sleep, cuddle with momma. I love them so much. They are my heart and lungs. Can you relate? I promise who they are at the core won't change in a few years when they become teens. My husband and I are so darn successful, but the one thing I can't buy them is white skin. And the ironic thing is that I've personally never learned any black history. My whole life I went to Catholic school, and *I'm* the one who is supposed to teach them why they should love their race? Ha! I'm lost myself, and although I desperately want a daughter, I shudder at the thought of being her role model.

Is there any country where I can go to be free of these thoughts that take over so much of my brain, robbing me from thinking happy thoughts about my children and their futures, their graduations and weddings? Is there some place I could move to and not be afraid of having another child for fear of their future? Because I definitely want another child so bad, but I refuse to bring another child into this world. Not another brown baby; my nerves can't handle it. Will America hate my babies? We have little interest in sports for them but would rather see them in medicine or engineering; is there still room for them in America? So nope, not another baby. Have you ever had these thoughts? I honestly may never let them go to regular school...they will probably be screwed up because this is so irrational, but is it? I was watching a Donald Trump rally today, and during the speech a few protestors were escorted out. Can you believe that seeing all those white faces in the crowd shouting "all lives matter" along with Donald shook me? I was surprised at my response because I'm not political at all, but it was so visceral! I'm sure it had to do with the KKK story being discussed all day today. There was so much hate in their eyes, mockery in their voices. For a moment I became afraid of the white faces in the audience; then I became afraid of whites in general, even my friends. Crazy, I know. I've never been a slave (obviously!), but the terror I felt in that moment made me wonder about the studies that say fear can be passed down genetically. I looked at my baby's sweet face and then wanted to puke. Irrational, I know, especially considering most of my friends are white—but I could never, ever share these thoughts with them, afraid to be cast away into the group of "other." I want to talk to you so badly, because I really need you right now. I need a friend. I never told you this, but I'm so sick of introducing myself to new whites by telling them that I'm a doctor before I tell them anything else about myself. It gets so old. When will being just me be enough? It's important for me that people make the distinction that I'm different, not like those "black lives matter" people on TV. But in actuality, what's so wrong with those people? They have a story to tell, but it doesn't matter now, because somehow their movement has a negative connotation, which is so far from the original intent. Wait a minute—I guess I should be saying "my" movement. To those who say, don't leave the country, stay and teach others, be a part of the solution, I say, "Please give me your white skin, just for one day." I want to know what it feels like to be free, really free of all the thoughts that invade and torment my mind. Switch with me for one day; then comment on this thread, and counsel me otherwise. When you post that you feel so bad, or post "hugs," or post that you empathize despite the fact that you've never had any similar concerns, I want to yell, "Please switch with me for one day!" I so desperately want to know what it feels like to empathize and not have ever had these thoughts.

Please pray that God gives me peace of mind and that America gives my children grace. I am exhausted. I am raw and pouring out my heart, so please, please, if you don't have anything constructive to say, please scroll past to the next thread. My

heart can't take any more. I probably rambled a bit, but that's what we do sometimes, right? Thank you for sticking with me, if you've read to the end.
—Heartbroken Mom

CHAPTER 1

Racism or "Relate-ism"?

* * *

MERRIAM-WEBSTER DEFINES *RACISM* AS "a belief that race is the primary determinant of human traits and capacities and that racial differences produce an inherent superiority of a particular race" and as "racial prejudice or discrimination."[2] The same dictionary defines *to relate* as "to show or make a connection between (two or more things)" and "to understand and like or have sympathy for someone or something."[3] The dictionary defines *ism* as "a distinctive doctrine, cause, or theory."[4]

---

2 Merriam-Webster.com, s.v. "Racism," accessed October 19, 2016, https://www.merriam-webster.com/dictionary/racism.

3 Merriam-Webster.com, s.v. "Relate," accessed October 19, 2016, https://www.merriam-webster.com/dictionary/relate.

4 Merriam-Webster.com, s.v. "Ism," accessed October 19, 2016, https://www.merriam-webster.com/dictionary/ism.

Throughout grade school, I and many other kids across the United States faced the same decision every day when we were determining where to sit in the school cafeteria. The decision was not a very difficult one to make, since an abundance of seats and tables was always available, and perhaps that made an otherwise simple decision difficult. Should I sit at one of the black tables, white tables, Asian tables, or Hispanic tables? The decision didn't stop there, though, because every one of these groups of tables had a subgroup of tables: the popular table, the athlete table, the goth table, the nerd table, and the I-don't-fit-anywhere-else table. The school had a table for everyone.

At a young age, I pondered whether these predominantly single-race tables existed because all the kids refused to break bread with kids from other races, or was something deeper going on? Deciding where to sit was instinctive for most kids, meaning that they put little forethought into the decision. Like most of my classmates, despite having friends spread across almost every table, each day I sat at one of the black tables, since these were the kids I could best relate to and who could best relate to me. Who would have guessed that many years later I would use this childhood observation to explain the concept of racism versus "relate-ism?" What I call relate-ism is the subconscious practice of identifying and associating with people you relate to, which then generates a host of other assumptions and biases about people you do not.

When I find myself in a situation where race could be a factor in my treatment, I remember my school-cafeteria observation and then first ask myself, "Is it racism I'm experiencing or relate-ism?"

* When I apply for a job, does the hiring manager make a conscious decision not to hire me because of my skin color, even though I'm the most qualified applicant? Perhaps he selects the less-qualified but more relatable applicant—an applicant whom he can envision attending the company golf outing or whom he would feel comfortable around his wife and kids?

* Does my boss have to warm up to me because he's racist or because he can't relate to me as easily as he can relate to others who do not share my skin color?

* Does the store greeter pretend that he doesn't see me (despite greeting and offering sales flyers to all the nonblack people coming into the store) because he's racist or because he can't relate to me as a black consumer?

Relate-ism, of course, doesn't always explain the mistreatment of black people; instead, you have to call it what it is, and that's outright racism. This is a good segue to an essay that Roger Guffey, a math and Sunday school teacher, wrote for the *Lexington Herald Leader* titled "You Just Might Be a Racist If..."

Psychologists have long recognized rationalization as a defense mechanism that people use to excuse unacceptable or offensive behaviors by offering some pseudo-logical reasoning or self-serving explanations.

Perhaps we justify that sumptuous dessert because we have earned a reward for sticking to our diet. Or we tell our boss we are sick, when we really want to go to the last game of the season. Some of these excuses are harmless, but far too often they are not.

For the last eight years, people who have mounted despicable attacks on President Obama and his family have tried to rationalize their bigotries. Consider these examples.

A Republican candidate here in Kentucky won a legislative seat, even though he had posted images of the Obama family as a band of monkeys, but he says he is not a racist.

Yes, you are.

A public official in West Virginia said she will be glad to have a dignified white first lady, instead of seeing an ape in high heels. But she says she is not a racist.

Yes, you are.

In Sheridan, Ind., people made a parade float of President Obama in a toilet, but said they are not racists.

Yes, you are.

A mayor in Pennsylvania ran a picture of Michele Obama on a wagon of orangutans under the caption "Move-in day at the White House," but denied being a racist.

Yes, you are.

The people who insist that President Obama is not a native-born American deny they are racists.

Yes, you are.

A candidate in Tennessee posted a billboard with the caption MAKE AMERICA WHITE AGAIN, but he denied that he is a racist.

Yes, you are.

A mayor in Washington State ran an image of Michelle Obama as a gorilla, saying she could be attractive only to another monkey like her husband. Of course, he says he is not a racist.

Yes, you are.

When a gorilla escaped from a zoo in South Carolina, a GOP politician in South Carolina posted a Facebook page telling people to be on the lookout for Michelle Obama's ancestor, but he says he is not racist.

Yes, you are.

After the 2008 election, some right-wing extremists circulated bumper stickers, quoting Psalm 109, that pray for God to kill President Obama, leaving his wife a widow and his children orphans, but they denied they are racists.

Yes, you are.

One of my favorite Abraham Lincoln stories relates his encounter with an elitist lawyer who, during a trial, dismissed him as a rustic bumpkin. Lincoln posed him a simple riddle. "If we call a tail a leg, how many legs does a horse have?" The smug lawyer replied, "Five." Lincoln corrected him. "No, he still has four legs, because calling a tail a leg does not make it one."

People are free to engage in self-delusion if they wish, but if it walks like a duck, quacks like a duck and swims like a duck, it is a duck, and these comments are racist. But perhaps these bigots should heed the poet Robert Burns' advice in the poem "To a Louse."

O would some power the gift give us to see ourselves as others see us.[5]

---

5 Roger Guffey, "You Just Might Be a Racist If..." *Lexington Herald Leader,* November 12, 2016, accessed December 12, 2016, http://www.kentucky.com/opinion/op-ed/article117123318.html.

One thing every black person should take from this article is that racist people do not walk around wearing "I am a racist" T-shirts. They don't look a certain way, they don't talk a certain way, nor do they come from a certain social class. Instead, they're often well-educated men and women in business suits or professional uniforms who are similar to the men and women you encounter every day in the workplace. You pass them in the hallways, you sit across from them in meetings, and some you call a friend. They may not openly mistreat you, but because of implicit bias, many don't see you as their equal. Many don't see you at all.

Racial discrimination still exists in corporate America; I've experienced it directly and have witnessed racism inflicted on others who share my skin color. My first introduction to institutional racial discrimination occurred during my sophomore year in college while I was working at a now-defunct department store whose logo was an oval with the store name written inside it. The store hired me to work at the checkout counter, but when it was short-staffed, I covered the customer-service desk. One afternoon while I was filling in at the customer-service desk, I came across a stack of employment applications. Curiosity got the best of me, so I thumbed through the stack of applications, looking for the names of college friends who might have needed me to put in a good word on their behalf.

What jumped out at me was that someone had blacked out the oval shaped store logo on some of the applications but not on others. My first thought was that someone who was working the customer-service desk had been doodling while bored. As I continued to thumb through the stack of applications, a disturbing pattern emerged. Someone blacked out the ovals on applications with ethnic-sounding names or applicants who had home addresses on the predominantly black side of town. I don't quite remember how this discovery made me feel, but since I've never been one to hold my tongue, I scheduled a meeting with the store manager to share my findings. The store manager's nonchalant demeanor was off-putting—almost as if she was in on the discriminatory scheme to weed out certain applicants. Not long after meeting with her, my hours began to dwindle until it became a waste of my time and effort to maintain employment. The memory of this experience never left me. It taught me, however, that organized corporate racism is very much alive and well.

CHAPTER 2

Black Paranoia

* * *

To be black in America is to be paranoid.

I have two life wishes. My first life wish is to know and fulfill God's plan for my life with the remaining time I have left on earth. Even without knowing what those plans are, I'm certain that the plans I have for myself pale in comparison to the plans He has for me. When my time on earth expires, how I will have died will not matter as much as how I lived, and I desire to live a life of purpose.

For many years, I've stood on Matthew 7:7–8 (NIV), God's promise that if I seek, I will find: "Ask and it will be given to you; seek and you will find; knock and the door will be opened to you. For everyone who asks receives; the one who seeks finds; and to the one who knocks, the door will be opened."

Asking God to reveal His plan for my life has been a lesson in patience. Unless I somehow missed His reply, I'm still awaiting an answer, which leaves me to wonder if my wish is unreasonable. Maybe I'm not supposed to know the plan for my life, because knowing might defeat the purpose of living. If I knew, then what would happen next? Would I cease to exist? Perhaps these questions are my attempt to pass the time while waiting for an answer.

My second life wish is to live for one day without experiencing a reminder of my skin color. Let me be clear: my wish is not for three days or even two days, only twenty-four hours free of black paranoia. Black paranoia is a made-up term for the obsession or strong belief that being black takes precedence over everything I do, every word I say, every decision I make, and every interaction I have with others. Below are several real black-paranoia moments I may experience in the course of a typical day.

- Did the store greeter fail to speak to my wife and me while cheerfully greeting the couples directly before and after us because we're black?
- Is store security following me because I'm black?
- If I purposely use casual language at work such as "ain't got" (as many of my nonblack coworkers do), will those in earshot assume that, unlike the others, I don't have a good grasp of the English language because I'm black?
- Did I not get the job because I'm black?
- Did I get the job because I'm black?

* Will my son receive less attention in school because he's black?
* Will my boss, peers, staff, or coworkers exaggerate a simple disagreement because I'm black?

The exhaustion of black-paranoia continues.

* Do people use slang when they talk to me because I'm black? It's interesting to hear the same people speak differently when they talk to others.
* Did the school provider describe my infant son's behavior as angry because my son is black? What's the difference between an angry infant and an upset infant? For black kids, the negative labels start early.
* Do my boss, peers, and coworkers lower their expectations of me because I'm black?
* Why do people often say that I "speak well"? Is being articulate an anomaly when you're black?

Pause to take a deep breath. I'm almost done.

* Did three business owners just last year (2016) refuse to provide my wife and me service because we are black? There were four business owners, in fact, but the owner of an arborist business admitted his discomfort providing services to someone of my skin color.

✦ Is it because my wife is black that restaurant staff passed her over multiple times while handing a rose to every other woman on Mother's Day? She stood in plain sight holding our infant son in his car seat. So much for making Mother's Day brunch reservations well in advance.

✦ Do nonblacks believe or even care that black lives matter? Cruelty to animals and an executive order travel ban receive widespread protest, and outrage. The senseless shootings of unarmed black men or the manmade disaster poisoning water for thousands of kids and families in predominantly black Flint, MI receive radio silence.

✦ Why do many nonblacks believe Black Lives Matter is synonymous for no other lives matter? If after stubbing your big toe, you say my big toe matters, is the automatic assumption the other four toes do not?

✦ Do people find it hard to believe that my wife is a physician because she's black?

People often inquire about what my wife does for a living. When I tell them she's a doctor, the typical response is, "Really?" or "How long has she been a physician assistant / physical therapist / nurse / another medical profession other than a doctor?" Either my wife or I will say that she's a board-certified doctor. This happens so frequently that it's become an inside joke (and sometimes even a bet) between the two of us when we're attending a function or other event. The bet has two parts: (1) How long will it take someone to ask what we do for a living? (2) After disclosing our professions, what medical profession besides doctor will others assume that they heard her say?

Black people know firsthand the mental and emotional toll of black paranoia. If you're black and you're reading this book, then you've already had several black-paranoia moments today; if you haven't, then you will before the day is over. Black paranoia doesn't happen by choice, because in the rare moments in which we receive a break from our skin color, someone will say or do something—or sometimes say or do nothing, such as ignoring us—to bring our skin color back into focus. Black skin can be exhausting, because we must remain mindful of what we do and say— activities others take for granted. Here are a few examples.

* Whenever I'm walking through a store and holding items I intend to purchase, my hands instinctively remain above my waist so that the items are visible at all times. I never want store employees, or even store patrons, to assume that I'd even consider shoving an unpaid item in my pockets.
* To avoid the stigma that I'm expecting a handout or a freebie, I never accept a restaurant's offer to compensate a meal or other item to make up for

poor customer service. If the manager or server insist and removes the item from the bill, then I include the price of the removed item with the tip I'd already intended to leave.

 * I've bought and sold many real-estate properties over the years. Regardless of the price point, when it was time to sell, I removed all traces of my racial identity, such as family photos, books, magazines, art, and CDs and DVDs. Yes, some buyers won't buy a house previously inhabited by a black person or family.

 * When I have questions at work, my boss, peers, or anyone else in my immediate organization are my last stops for answers. Why? Because when black professionals ask questions, our "not knowing" speaks to a perceived shortcoming; not knowing something serves as an indictment of our intelligence or ability to comprehend and follow directions.

Most black professionals are familiar with the "You mean you don't know that?" facial expression we often receive when we ask a question in the workplace. Because, of course, everyone but us presumably already know the answer to any question we ask. In contrast, our nonblack counterparts who ask questions others see as being mature, since doing so shows the ability to recognize the limitations of their understanding and the use of resources to fill in any gaps.

Whenever black people hear nonblack leaders proclaim to see their staff as family, we know the statement does not include us. The statement may sound noble, and the person who's making the statement may mean well, but the reality is that workplaces across the United States have made it clear by their actions (not their words) that this family-affair is for nonblacks only.

The black paranoia we experience outside the workplace is mentally and emotionally exhausting. Compound that exhaustion with the mental and emotional exhaustion that black professionals experience in the workplace, and for many, surviving eight or more hours of work each day with our sanity still intact is a herculean accomplishment.

CHAPTER 3

The Best Advice

* * *

W HENEVER YOU WALK INTO A room, the assumptions and biases that other people have of you walk in first. When people first catch sight of a black person, they form assumptions and examine the biases they hold of other black people. Members of other racial backgrounds also suffer from negative assumptions and biases, so that part is not unique; the uniqueness is that black professionals do not get a chance to make a first impression. The assumptions and biases that others have of us permanently define who we are. In a microcosmic work environment, these assumptions and biases reverberate and are infectious.

At every job I've held, a nonblack person has advised me to avoid at least one black person because of his or her unfavorable reputation; because I like to get off to a good start at any job, I heeded the advice. Whenever these black exiles were close by, I would walk in the opposite direction. If interaction with them was unavoidable, then I would do whatever it took to make sure their transgressions didn't rub off on me. Despite these and other precautionary measures, I still couldn't shake my curiosity about their workplace crimes, though. While maintaining a generous distance, I'd continue to observe them so that I could better understand whatever egregious actions they'd done to seal their workplace fate. I took copious notes.

One day while thumbing through years of compiled notes of the many black professionals that nonblacks advised me to avoid, a common theme jumped out at me. In each case, these black professionals had made someone in the workplace uncomfortable because of the double standard of corporate America. While others in the workplace might be considered passionate, a black professional's passion is considered aggression, which makes others uncomfortable. While someone else in the workplace might be considered outspoken, the black professional's outspokenness is considered insubordination or rudeness, which makes others uncomfortable. While someone else in the workplace might be considered a go-getter, the black professional who does the same is stepping on toes or challenging authority, which makes others uncomfortable.

The workplace double standard has resulted in the permanent labeling of these black professionals, many of whom eventually move on. As a result, job-hopping is common among black professionals, but it shouldn't be.

While the names, faces, and employers may change, the overall frustrations and challenges that black professionals encounter in the workplace remain the same. Early in my career, this was one of the hardest lessons for me to learn. I'd convinced myself that the next job or the next boss would be different, but they rarely were. It was like hitting the repeat button.

People often seek my advice about whether leaving their current jobs would be the right thing to do, and my response is always the same: Do you want to leave for a better opportunity, or are you running away from someone or something? This question has no value if we don't give it an honest and introspective answer. Since none of us can outrun our blackness, whatever you're running from in your current job will be waiting for you at your next job.

Besides, sometimes value can be found in putting up with the nonsense you know versus leaving for unknown nonsense that could be twice as bad. If you must leave, then you should always leave for the right reasons. Never leave before you've invested in yourself, whether that's job experience, a degree or certification, or specialized training. Time is nonrefundable, so make the challenges and frustrations you endure on each job count for something positive.

Remain wary of those in the workplace (or anywhere) who proclaim that they don't see your skin color. Their claim is not only disingenuous but also insulting to the many black men and women who know firsthand that there's no place in the United States where our skin color goes unnoticed.

We all see skin color. Anyone who tells you otherwise only wants you to drop your guard and relax; this is a luxury black people lack, since they must be "on", "guarded", and "un" at all times: un-intimidating, un-threatening, un-angry, and as un-black as possible. Claiming not to see skin color is the same as saying that this country doesn't have a race and inequality problem. A narrative of many people who believe that racial inequality disappeared with the election of Barack Obama as president of the United States a few years back.

Skin color is always at the forefront. Take the following examples.

* A Cheerios commercial depicting an interracial family comprising a black man, a white woman, and an adorable interracial little girl drew hostility and outrage on the Internet. People saw color, and they were outraged!

* An Old Navy commercial depicting another interracial family comprising a black woman, a white man, and a little boy caused an uproar in which people accused Old Navy of white genocide and anti-white propaganda. People saw color, and they were outraged!

* In 2014, Maserati aired a Super Bowl commercial for a high-end luxury car that featured the up-and-coming young black actress Quvenzhané Wallis. The Internet erupted in outrage!

* Let's not forget how the Internet became unhinged when the movie *The Hunger Games* cast two black actors for the characters of Rue and Thresh (Suzanne Collins's book *Mockingjay* describes both characters as having dark skin). The movie stayed true to the best-selling novel that inspired it, but this fact didn't quell the outpouring of criticism by some of the author's fans, who seemingly couldn't come to grips with those two main characters' being black. Again, the supposedly colorblind people were outraged!

* While I was working as a waiter in college, a party of nine white guests refused me as their server because, as they told my manager, they didn't want a nigger around their food. Those people saw my skin color for sure!

These are just a few examples where skin color was the focal point. A quick search online; however, will yield many more examples involving companies—maybe yours among them—that made skin color such a focal point that a court found them guilty of racial discrimination. Despite countless examples, many companies expect black professionals to suspend everything they know to be true by believing that the workplace is a sanctuary: a retreat where their skin color will go unnoticed and where their bosses, peers, staff, and coworkers will view them as an equal. This is nonsense! I am not asserting that the people who surround black professionals are bad people; however, I believe it doesn't come natural for them to invest themselves in the professional growth and development of black professionals over those who share their skin color.

If you disagree, and believe your boss, peers, staff, and coworkers view you with an impartial and unbiased lens, then you have likely spent a lot of time ingratiating yourself in their good graces and very little time observing them. Even a moment of casual observation can reveal a great deal about how they feel about you, but first you must stop looking and listening for the smoking guns while ignoring the loud subtleties that happen all around you every day.

Expect no one in the workplace to reveal how they really feel about you: they may tell their husbands or wives and they may tell others in the workplace, but they'll never tell you. Get in the habit of evaluating those around you by their actions, not their words. Compare how they treat you with how they treat others who don't share your skin color. Compare the support they show you with the support they show others who don't share your skin color. Compare the opportunities they offer to you with the opportunities they offer to others who don't share your skin color. Here's a simple comparison. Compare the interaction your boss has with you with the interaction he or she has with others who do not share your skin color. What you observe will amaze you.

Although some observers have put forth proof that workplaces across the United States are hotbeds of racism, I don't believe this assessment is entirely accurate. Implicit biases, however—biases activated at the subconscious level—still create just as many frustrations and challenges for black professionals. The Kirwan Institute for the Study of Race and Ethnicity in Columbus, Ohio, describes implicit bias this way:

Implicit bias refers to the attitudes or stereotypes that affect our understanding, actions, and decisions in an unconscious manner. These biases, which encompass both favorable and unfavorable assessments, are activated involuntarily and without an individual's awareness or intentional control. Residing deep in the subconscious, these biases are different from known biases that individuals may choose to conceal for the purposes of social and/or political correctness. Rather, implicit biases are not accessible through introspection.[6]

The biases against black professionals in the workplace have far-reaching consequences, because the same people who harbor these biases against them are in positions to make decisions that can, and often do, negatively affect them. It is imperative to understand that a company having a diversity program is not the same as a company having a

---

6 "Understanding Implicit Bias," Kirwan Institute for the Study of Race and Ethnicity, accessed August 13, 2016, http://kirwaninstitute.osu.edu/research/understanding-implicit-bias/.

true commitment to recognizing diversity differences and creating a comfortable working environment for everyone. It's my belief that most diversity programs exist so that companies can check the "I have a diversity program" box.

Workplace diversity is much more than having people of various skin tones and genders sprinkled throughout the leadership ranks or even sitting around conference-room tables. True diversity is when those diverse people occupy decision-making positions instead of being mere seat-filling tokens. Companies have led many people in the workplace to believe that a diversity program is a pot-luck during Hispanic Heritage Month or a few quotes or sound bites from Dr. Martin Luther King Jr.'s "I Have a Dream" speech. Although there are benefits to both in certain situations, I wouldn't consider either as being diversity strengthening, enrichment or inclusion.

Despite the rhetoric of numerous Silicon Valley CEOs about wanting diverse workforces, recruiting black talent remains paltry in the high-tech sector. Some of the brightest minds in this country are solving some of the world's most complex problems using technology that was unfathomable just ten years ago, but increasing the recruitment and retention of black talent seemingly has these people stumped. Either their true intent is to exclude or minimize the hiring of certain racial groups, or these CEOs are not as smart as they would want us all to believe. If anyone who's reading this book truly desires some fresh ideas for increasing the hiring and retention of black talent, then please get in touch with me using the contact information listed in the front of the book.

The speaker at one training class on leadership I attended made a profound comment: "Everyone desires a sense of belonging in the workplace, and that sense of belonging is fundamental and the core of a harmonious workplace environment." While I agreed with his comment (and still do), I wondered whether he had given any thought to (or cared to understand) how difficult it is for black professionals to feel a sense of belonging in the workplace. To gain a deeper appreciation for the speaker's comment, I turned to Wikipedia, which describes *belongingness* as:

> the human emotional need to be an accepted member of a group. Whether it is family, friends, co-workers, a religion, or something else, people tend to have an "inherent" desire to belong and be an important part of something greater than themselves. This implies a relationship that is greater than simple acquaintance or familiarity.[7]

I, like many other black professionals, can't relate to feeling a sense of belonging in a workplace that disproportionately

---

7   Wikipedia, s.v. "Belongingness," accessed May 12, 2016, https://en.wikipedia.org/w/index.php?title=Belongingness&oldid=749597073.

represents black professionals. In one engineering or management position after the next, in one boardroom meeting after the next, in one business lunch after the next, I see few or no black faces looking back at me. On every job, I have a dual responsibility. I am responsible for the transgressions of every black person that came before me, and I am responsible for blazing a trail for every black person who comes after me to follow. Twice I was the highest-ranked or most senior black professional in the company; while to some this would be a reason to gloat, for me, all hope vanished that one day I might cross paths with a black peer who'd be able to relate to me.

It's difficult to feel a sense of belonging in a workplace where the slightest elevation of my voice, subtle furrow in my brow, or manifestation of a strong personality, often intimidates my boss, peers, staff, and coworkers. As a result, many black professionals and I become simple acquaintances or merely familiar faces to others in the workplace. Bosses will often use these simple acquaintance relationships against blacks, however, in favor of providing mentorship, leadership development, and other opportunities to the nonblack people they know well.

Instead of feeling a sense of belonging in the workplace, others' words and actions (and sometimes inactions, such as ignoring them), often make black professionals feel that they do not belong. They watch from the sidelines as their bosses, peers, and coworkers cultivate relationships with those who do not share their skin color. Yet, and despite being relegated to the sidelines, the workplace expectation is that during work-related social events, black professionals will partake and feel comfortable around the same people who feel uncomfortable around them. Choosing not to partake only serves to validate the assumptions and biases of black people being anti-social and unfriendly in the workplace.

CHAPTER 4

What's Wrong with You?

* * *

BLACK PROFESSIONALS HAVE AN EXTRA responsibility to make the men and women who surround us and who often have no regard for our comfort feel comfortable at all times

I've always considered myself a friendly person, so I never understood why, early in my career, bosses frequently advised me to smile more or asked me what was wrong. I can remember receiving an end-of-the-year performance evaluation that included the words "Needs to smile more" in the Additional Comments section—a comment that today I'd find inappropriate, since it has nothing to do with my job performance. To a young and naive college graduate, however, smiling more sounded like great advice for anyone. Besides, I was of the belief that corporate America comprised eager men and women of various racial backgrounds who were ready to mentor me and guide me down the path of corporate success; any advice they might give me therefore would be in my best interest.

Whenever I received this advice to smile more, I made the necessary adjustments so that I could morph into the workplace Cheshire Cat. I was smiling for the sake of smiling, but it came at a price: sore facial muscles, frequently cracked lips, and overall disingenuous facial expressions. The charade continued until the facial discomfort became too much to tolerate, which forced a return to my authentic, but not good enough, self.

Over time, I began studying the facial expressions of nonblack employees in meetings, hallways, the cafeteria, the parking garage—everywhere, really. What I observed only added to my confusion and frustration; they weren't smiling more than I or any other blacks in the workplace were. They were actually smiling much less, yet others saw them as being pleasant and approachable, which were two characteristics that I thought described me (but evidently didn't). My confusion and frustration lingered for many years until one day I received an opportunity to peek inside the mind of a supervisor who, like the others, advised me to smile more and frequently asked me what was wrong. "Let's call him Kevin".

Kevin and I developed a workplace friendship that grew out of our love for professional sports (mainly football). Besides engaging in topics about which NFL players were rising or falling in our fantasy football league or the players poised to have a breakout game, when we were alone we also discussed topics commonly viewed as taboo to discuss in the workplace, such as politics, religion, or race. Kevin was the perfect person to illuminate what had perplexed me for years. One evening after wrapping up a taboo discussion on politics, I seized the moment and asked Kevin why he so often advised me to smile more or asked me what was wrong.

He replied, "Why do you ask?"

After I explained my desire to gain a deeper understanding of the advice that he and previous bosses had given me, Kevin hesitated for what seemed like an eternity and said, "Are you sure you want to know?"

"Of course," I replied, although his long hesitation made me uncertain that I was ready to hear what he had to say.

"Whenever I pass you in the hall or observe you in meetings," he finally said, "you often appear upset, as if something's bothering you."

While I appreciated Kevin's answer, I wanted more details—starting with how my face reflected me being upset and bothered. I continued to probe him by asking, "Do I walk around frowning?"

Kevin replied with an emphatic no and continued, "It's difficult to explain how you sometimes look."

I didn't press him for more information after I noticed a sudden change in his demeanor and body language. Although I'd hoped for a substantive discussion, I was grateful to be a step closer to cracking the "Smile more" and "What's wrong?" code. Unfortunately, it would take a few more years and a casual conversation with my mentor before I'd gain a deeper understanding.

Some people are inherently uncomfortable around black people, and being educated, well spoken, and well-groomed does little to quell their discomfort, I remember my mentor saying. To be more specific, he said that my dark skin, tallness, athletic build, tone of voice, bald head, and even my displays of confidence might invoke fear or make others perceive a threat where there was none. He suggested that their discomfort could have been due to a variety of reasons, but it was usually the result of consciously or even subconsciously evaluating me through their assumptions and biases about black people.

Often when people evaluate their assumptions and biases, they end up substantiating their own preconceived beliefs. The recurring advice to smile more and the frequently asked question of what was wrong had nothing to do with what Kevin and others *saw* but instead how my presence made Kevin and others *feel*.

This revelation was my first introduction to the secondary responsibility of every black professional: *we must make the men and women who surround us and who often have no regard for our comfort feel comfortable at all times.* Many people in the workplace view black professionals as volatile, so advising us to smile more is the same as asking us to at all times provide a visual indicator of our mood, emotions, or state of mind. The assumption is that a smiling black person is happy, content, and disarming, whereas a black person who is not smiling is alarming and cause for concern—serious concern to some, because the potential for volatility is real. This overdue discussion knocked the naïveté out of me and changed me from an eager college graduate with grandiose plans and expectations for corporate America bliss to a black man standing in front of a precipitous corporate America cliff.

Fast-forward to the present, and the same logic can help explain (but not justify) what has been this country's secret for decades until recently, thanks to the popularity of smartphones, GoPro, and various other mobile-recording devices: the frequent police shootings of unarmed black men. I do not agree with the popular belief that racist police officers or rampant racism in police departments across the United States are the primary cause for these senseless killings. Rather, these officers' trigger-happy behavior stems from the same intrinsic fear of black people that they share with those we encounter in the workplace daily. One elevated voice, one furrowed brow, or one slight movement deemed too aggressive or threatening and police officers will respond according to their training, which is to eliminate the threat.

The same applies to the work environment; the only difference is that a pen and paper (and often covertly organized collusion) in corporate America replaces the guns used by police officers on the streets. I respect police officers across the country for their bravery and services, and I believe that anyone convicted of killing an officer in uniform, regardless of race, should face the maximum penalty allowed by law. Similarly, we should not simply sweep under the rug the killing of an unarmed black person—or any person, for that matter—by a police officer.

If it's so easy for black professionals' mere presence at work to make their coworkers feel uncomfortable and threatened, then why would police officers be any different? People often view black people as a threat in the streets and a threat in corporate seats. I'm thankful that most workplaces in the United States forbid the carrying of firearms, or else black professionals could be on a path to extinction.

It doesn't take much for others to feel threatened by a black person; sometimes it takes nothing at all. I remember once that I needed to discuss a sensitive topic with a coworker (whom I also considered a friend), so I suggested that we meet at a nearby coffee shop, away from listening ears. The discussion took less than ten minutes, and because it was close to lunch, we grabbed a bite to eat before we headed back to the office. Over the many months that followed, I had no reason to believe that not all was well, since our interactions at work and outside work were the same as they had always been. He was no different from the friend I'd always known him to be.

That changed when months later he became disgruntled with me and described the meeting at the coffee shop as being contentious and hostile. I was at a lost for words; his recollection of our meeting left me speechless. There is a critical lesson that every black person should glean from this experience. Many nonblacks are not above pulling the "scary black person" card when it works to their advantage. This person's actions reflect who he is (and has always been) at his core. You'll read more about his deceptive behavior in chapters 7 and 8.

As I've moved along in my career, the advice to smile more and the frequency of being asked what's wrong have both subsided, but the discomfort my skin color seems to cause others has remained a constant. The discomfort of my presence manifests itself in many ways. The following examples are my personal experiences; however, many black professionals reported experiencing the same.

Few days go by when I don't feel like a zombie on The Walking Dead because of how my presence causes others to look the other way, drop their head, or summon superhuman powers to flatten themselves against the hallway wall to avoid speaking or making eye contact with me. There is nothing more amusing, but at the same time alienating, than to witness someone say "good morning" to the three people walking directly ahead of me, skip me, and say "good morning" to the two people walking directly behind me. My blackness makes me question the motives behind the selective display of professional courtesy. When this happens, I go the extra mile to acknowledge their presence, and the best part is the manufactured, startled, "oh, I didn't see you?" look.

Some people in the workplace expect a heated exchange when they're speaking with me, so instead of having a meaningful dialogue, they prefer to speak only when I'm speaking. My experiences don't include those who are socially awkward or those who have poor workplace etiquette but rather those that I observe having respectful and patient dialogues when speaking with others but who can only have high-energy monologues with me as I fight to get a word in. The trap is set because fighting too hard to get a word in results in accusations of arguing and hostility.

Another manifestation of discomfort is the scrunched "I don't understand the words that are coming out of your mouth" facial expression I often receive when speaking to some people in the workplace. I am left wondering if I've failed to convey my point or perhaps my point couldn't penetrate closed ears that assumed what I had to say was not worth hearing.

Another is the experience of speaking to someone who has to defer to someone else to help explain what I had just finished saying. Once the interpreter translates black English to intelligible English, the scrunched facial expression becomes a much-needed sigh of relief. The reaction to blacks when they communicate in corporate America often swings from one extreme to another: people either show surprise when they exhibit proficiency in the English language or they rush to find an interpreter because they speak so poorly.

I've had peers who during meetings, take whatever I say and present it back to the other meeting attendees in their own words, preceded by something like, "I think this is what you're trying to say, but please correct me if I'm wrong." It seems when they were around I was always *trying* to communicate.

Bosses are often the worst at hiding their discomfort around me; this can be most apparent during one-on-one interactions, where their inability to relax is difficult to mask. Moments of casual conversation or meaningless banter can seem forced; their body language can seem guarded, uptight, and tense; and their genuine interest in me seem manufactured.

The most amusing displays of discomfort and uneasiness often occur in meetings with a VIP or distinguished guest. I raise my hand to ask a question, and the room becomes so quiet you can hear a gnat urinating on a cotton ball. I take a few seconds to scan the room and absorb the "Why is he even here?", "Uh oh, what is he about to say?", or the "Please don't embarrass us" looks on the faces in the crowd. Take a deep breath. I am a black professional, and I fully understand my additional responsibility, which is to make the men and women around me—many of whom have little regard for my comfort—feel comfortable at all times.

CHAPTER 5

The Benefit of
the Doubt

* * *

EVERY DAY ON THE JOB is a black professional's first day
on the job.

Giving someone the benefit of the doubt means as-
suming that a person or fact is correct or justified until you can prove the contrary. By this definition, black
professionals shouldn't expect to receive the benefit of
the doubt in the workplace, because unlike our nonblack
counterparts, the workplace often assumes that black professionals are guilty (or at least part of the problem) until
proven otherwise. Black professionals must therefore remain vigilant and ready to defend themselves, sometimes
at a moment's notice. If you find yourself in the workplace
crosshairs, your blemish-free work history won't matter,
your accolades and accomplishments won't matter, and
who you know won't matter, because every day on the job

is a black professional's first day on the job. The workplace often won't afford you the benefit of the doubt, so your ability to use every resource at your disposal to defend yourself against mistreatment from bosses, peers, staff, and coworkers is critical.

If you ever find yourself on the receiving end of baseless allegations or mistreatment, your boss will declare his or her intentions to perform a full and impartial investigation. However, assumptions and biases because of your skin color mean that the investigation will often start from your assumed guilt. Allow your boss unpressured time to investigate, but do not put your workplace fate solely in the hands of your boss.

To share a personal story, a peer of mine once made an insensitive remark about the mental health of a staff member who had recently attempted suicide while at work. After I sternly asked this person to leave my office, he shoved me against the wall and made another insensitive remark. I instinctively responded by shoving him twice as hard and following up with a few colorful words. He returned the colorful words, which resulted in a chest-to-chest standoff, although no fight ensued. Word of the altercation made its way to our boss, who called me into his office for questioning. He said, "You know he's an asshole, so why'd you let him provoke you?" I couldn't argue with my boss's assessment, nor could I say why I'd failed to maintain my self-control.

I had a much greater concern, though: After the boss had heard the facts from those who'd witnessed the confrontation, would the asshole walk away unscathed while I face some form of punitive actions? My boss seemed offended by my concern and with an elevated voice said, "What kind of company do you think we run around here? Do you think I'd give him a slap on the wrist and send you to the guillotine?" In my head, I yelled a resounding yes, but instead I said, "Good to hear." A week later, the boss announced in an email that the other person had received a promotion. My punishment, although not so severe as a guillotine blade slamming against the back of my neck, was severe enough to feel the breeze from the blade as it dropped.

For many black professionals, only two facts seem to matter in the workplace:

* Fact #1: We are black and therefore are more likely to be the antagonists and aggressors.
* Fact #2: Our accusers are not black and are therefore assumed to be the helpless victims.

The fact that black professionals are not in leadership positions with decision-making authority means that the likelihood of someone who is black being in a position to oversee fairness and objectivity in the workplace is nonexistent. Instead, the people who are responsible for addressing the concerns of black professionals are often the same people who share many of the widespread assumptions and biases about them, thus making fairness, objectivity, and benefit of the doubt nearly impossible to receive. If black professionals have problems or concerns in the workplace, they often hear things such as:

* They are being too sensitive.
* Others didn't take offense, so neither should they.
* They should make more of an effort to get to know the offending parties.
* That is just how the offending parties are. As if knowing this additional piece of information will make the offensive behavior acceptable.

Take a moment to digest the automatic assumption in all four responses. The problems that black professionals often face in the workplace result from something that they are, or are not, doing. Adjusting themselves will thus eliminate the problem, because the thought of a boss, peer, staff member, or coworker acting on their assumptions and biases of black people based on their skin color would seem to be impossible. The benefit of the doubt shown to nonblacks means there has to be a legitimate reason why someone would rather work alone on a labor-intensive assignment or task than to work with a black person. This is a common experience for black people in the workplace and academia.

Many times my boss asked me to work with a person or a team who, by their words, actions, body language, or lack of engagement, didn't want to work with me. Many lied and proclaimed that I contributed when I hadn't. I found over the years that sharing these concerns with my boss would only confirm the boss's assumptions and biases that I don't work well with others. Sharing these concerns with the person or team involved only confirmed their assumptions and biases that I am argumentative and contentious. Doing nothing only confirmed the collective assumptions and biases that I was looking for a handout. This is just one of many situations in which black professionals do not receive the benefit of the doubt in the workplace.

Nonblack professionals often receive the benefit of the doubt even when that benefit of the doubt is undeserved. There must be a good reason why she unleashed a verbal assault during a staff meeting. Or he must have marital problems, family problems, financial problems, health problems, pet problems, drinking problems, gambling problems, erectile-dysfunction problems, or some other personal problem that would help to explain why he'd behaved so out of character. I've heard all these excuses and more for defending the unprofessional behavior of nonblack employees.

In contrast, no excuses can help explain the unprofessional behavior of black professionals. The most lopsided example I can think of is the reprimand of a black professional for engaging in a verbal altercation and a nonblack professional allowed permanent telecommuting privileges after engaging in a physical altercation. Both worked for the same company.

CHAPTER 6

Fixture or Accessory

* * *

If you don't have a plan for yourself, then you'll be part of someone else's plan; because you're black, that's no plan at all. This I guarantee.

Merriam-Webster defines an *accessory* as "a thing of secondary or subordinate importance."[8] It defines a *fixture* as "a familiar or invariably present element or feature in some particular setting."[9] If you were to apply these definitions to workplace dynamics, would you consider yourself a fixture or an accessory?

It's easy to tell the two apart but only if you know what to look for. The boss gives fixtures the authority to make decisions on his or her behalf; as a result, others in the workplace see the fixture as an extension of the boss or

8 Merriam-Webster.com, s.v. "Accessory," accessed June 21, 2016, https://www.merriam-webster.com/dictionary/accessory.
9 Merriam-Webster.com, s.v. "Fixture," accessed June 21, 2016, https://www.merriam-webster.com/dictionary/accessory.

as an "organizational change agent," to use a bit of workplace jargon. Fixtures receive meeting and conference call invitations because others value their opinions and have a genuine interest in what they have to say. Accessories also receive meeting and conference call invites, but their expectations are different from those of a fixture. Their role is for others to see them but not hear them.

When bosses are on leave, they'll leave fixtures in charge; the grooming of fixtures usually starts shortly after their arrival and occurs in plain sight. Should black professionals inquire why the boss never leaves them in charge, the boss will usually reply that they lack understanding on a particular topic or don't have a specific skill. While this may be true, black professionals should remember fixtures also lacked these skills before receiving mentoring and shown how to conduct business in the boss's absence. Black professionals should save their hopes and prayers on this subject, because it is unlikely that their bosses will ever do the same for them. The risk of leaving an intimidating and potentially ticking time bomb as the face of the company in the boss's absence is too great of a risk. Make no mistake about it, your boss and others know this.

I've known nonblack fixtures whom others in the workplace considered subject-matter experts on all things, but they lacked a fundamental understanding on the most basic information to be useful. I've also known just as many black accessories who possessed a breadth of knowledge across many disciplines but whom others dismissed as having little or nothing of significance to contribute.

At this stage in my career, I proudly fall into the latter category. Although, I continue to offer my input and help where needed, I no longer scratch and claw for my boss, peers, and coworkers to take my input seriously. Instead, I stand comfortably on the sidelines where I'm often pushed, and watch as the same people who consider themselves intellectually superior to me spin in circles to solve simple workplace problems. Despite their best efforts to manufacture a flair of confidence, many people can't hide their insecurities; as a result, their marginalization of my ideas and me has more to do with them and their shortcomings. To satisfy their need for relevancy, small workplace problems require multiple meetings, countless email exchanges, numerous hallway discussions, and a few more meetings before they'll arrive at the same solution that I—the accessory—arrived at weeks and sometimes months earlier.

Much like the jewelry accessories my wife wears to complement her attire, accessories are replaceable; to lose an accessory is no big deal. The impact of losing a fixture is much greater, however, because their value is proportional to the investment. Don't believe for a minute that overseeing a staff of people makes them accessories and you a fixture. It's usually quite the opposite; if you oversee a predominantly or completely nonblack staff, then others in the workplace will view you as having no value to add. Many black professionals have noticed that when their nonblack staff members fail, the cause of their failure is a lack of leadership and guidance from the black professional. When these same staff members succeed, then their success had nothing to do with the black professional. The black professional is excluded from all talks of their success.

To eliminate any confusion about whether you're a fixture or an accessory, tomorrow while you're at work, I challenge you to do something you may not have done before. Live in the moment and observe what you see and hear. Do you feel engaged? Do people seek your opinions? Do people invite you to meetings? Do people give you challenging tasks? Are you included in collaboration groups or brainstorming sessions? Does your boss take a genuine interest in you personally and professionally? Are you included in what's happening, or does your boss or a peer have to fill you in on what's already happened? Whom does your boss seek for advice or collaboration, you or your peers? After conducting what I hope was a thorough observation, ask yourself again; Am I a fixture or an accessory?

If you fall into the accessory zone, then you're not alone. It would seem that black professionals have a monopoly on the accessory zone. Some of my jobs that hired me to be a fixture eventually relegated me to accessory status; I don't know exactly when it happened, how it happened, or why it happened. At this stage in my career, being an accessory doesn't bother me the same way it might bother someone at the apex of his or her professional journey. Besides being further along in my career, I'm also a dad now, and success in that endeavor is much more important and gratifying to me than climbing the corporate ladder, receiving corporate recognition and awards, or chasing corporate dollars.

There's nothing wrong with starting out as an accessory as long as you're not content with remaining an accessory. I can't imagine the life I would lead now had I kept working at restaurants in high school; as enjoyable as those jobs were, they wouldn't have afforded me the life I have today. I learned early in life; *never settle for less because you'll always get less than what you settled for.*

If you're an accessory, then be the best accessory you can be. You also need to work on a move-up or move-on plan. Advancement in any field usually requires improving on a particular skill; now that the Internet is available on every desk and hip, an endless amount of training is just a few clicks away. Ask if your employer offers access to free computer-based training and/or e-books, since many do. A website I frequently use for free IT training is cybrary.com. After creating a free account, you'll have immediate access to an extensive list of the latest IT certifications and training videos, accessible from anywhere. YouTube and Google Books are excellent resources for free training videos and books, respectively. Two fee-based services that offer an assortment of training videos and books are Netflix and Amazon Prime. Finally, and only if it's financially feasible to do so, sign up for a night or weekend class at the local university or community college to earn credits toward a degree or certification. Your employer may offer full or partial tuition assistance to offset some or all of the costs.

Sometimes you do what you have to do until you can do what you want to do. A move-up or move-on plan doesn't always have to improve your current work situation. Your plan might include gaining new skills that will open doors in a different field of work. Maybe your plan is to start a business that will allow you to bid farewell to your nine-to-five job once the business grows into a steady stream of income. Your plan can be whatever you want it to be, just so long as it gets you closer to doing what you want to do. Remember to always have a plan for yourself, as I mentioned earlier. If you don't, then someone else will; if you're black, that's no plan at all.

I live in a perpetual mode of planning, so I always have a plan B. Here are a few of my plans that have either come to fruition or are on my to-accomplish list:

* Acquiring real-estate properties—check.
* Achieving a master's degree—check.
* Achieving various IT certifications—check.
* Starting a consulting business—check.
* Providing scholarships to underprivileged kids—check.
* Increasing public-speaking engagements—check.
* Launching various e-commerce businesses—check.
* Becoming a father—check.
* Multiple trademarks—in progress.
* Publishing my first book—in progress.

There's no time like the present, so work on your plan B today.

Only one area should concern you when dealing with your boss's treatment of fixtures, and this is a biggie. Bosses and others frequently assign fixtures extra duties and assignments and then use those extras to justify why the fixture is more deserving of recognition or a higher performance evaluation than you are, even though you gladly would've taken on more responsibility if anyone had asked. This is just one of many workplace tactics against black professionals.

CHAPTER 7

Black Tyranny

* * *

Show me a strong and confident black leader in the workplace, and I'll show you someone whom others see as a black tyrant.

During my journey in corporate America, I have not crossed paths with many blacks in leadership positions. When I did though, it has always been special for me. Instead of limiting myself to observing these rare sightings from afar, I set out to get to know them on a more personal level. My goal was to extract a golden nugget or two that might prove useful in my professional development. These leaders had many things in common—among them, confidence, humility, decisiveness, and focus. They also had one commonality that I found disturbing. At least once in their careers, staff members accused them of bullying and cultivating toxic and hostile work environments. Their stories were plausible and consistent; I'd heard many of their staff members use disparaging words to describe their bosses. In their eyes, their bosses were nothing more than titleholders devoid of any real value.

One such leader was Dr. "Kennedy", a retired army chief warrant officer. I remember Dr. Kennedy as a humble, family man with deep Christian beliefs. Besides earning his numerous military awards and commendations, Dr. Kennedy had also earned a master's degree and a doctorate in business administration. The first time Dr. Kennedy and I met for lunch, the conversation started with my rambling on about his many great life accomplishments. He cut me off midsentence when he said, "Past or future accomplishments will never cause me to puff out my chest." He could have responded to my ramblings by thanking me for the shower of compliments; instead, he wanted me to know that he didn't see himself as a big deal. I thought his statement was impressive.

There wasn't much complexity to the organizational structure; Dr. Kennedy was one of four branch chiefs who all reported to a single division chief. The division chief announced his departure soon after my arrival, so he and I didn't get to know each other well. What I noticed during our brief time together was his wild popularity. Here's one such example. Many employees arrived early to the weekly staff meetings to get a seat at the conference-room table where the division chief and the other branch chiefs sat. It was not just a seat at the conference-room table they were after, but also a seat as close to the division chief as possible.

Those who arrived on time or late to the meeting sat in the chairs along the perimeter of the conference-room wall; they watched in envy as others basked in the glow of the division chief.

The company announced its plans to hire someone from within to backfill the division-chief position, which meant a great opportunity for one lucky branch chief would soon be up for grabs. The consensus around the water cooler and throughout the hallways was that people preferred anyone but Dr. Kennedy. Many people questioned his ability to lead and his ability to carry out the division chief position duties. He is a black man so many people also questioned his temperament.

Much to everyone's surprise, including my own, the selection committee selected Dr. Kennedy for the division-chief position. The disappointment in the air following the announcement was palpable. The weekly staff meeting location and time remained the same, but there was one glaring difference. Remember how people arrived early to the staff meeting just to get a seat at the conference-room table closest to the division chief. The popularity of the conference-room table was no more with Dr. Kennedy at the helm. Almost every seat at the conference-room table was available, while the seats along the perimeter of the wall were all occupied. I couldn't hide the embarrassment I felt for Dr. Kennedy, who had yet to arrive. Would he see what I saw, would he share in my embarrassment and shame, or would he consider it another day in the life of a black leader? I'll never know because I was too embarrassed to follow-up with him.

Another such story is that of Colonel Glenda J. Lock of the US Army. The highlight of Colonel Lock's story is her staff accused her of trying to circumvent the "tape" portion of the army's physical fitness test. The process of being "taped" entails an evaluator wrapping a measuring tape around one's waist, bust, and hips to assess whether the circumferences fall within set army standards for one's gender and height. This wouldn't be much of a story if the allegations against Colonel Lock had stopped there, but she's black, and she's a woman, so they didn't. Additional comments from Colonel Lock's staff are as follows:

* She "tried to intimidate subordinates."
* She was an "authoritarian leader and sometimes [was an] abusive bully."
* She "decimated morale" and was "abrasive."
* She created a "poor command climate" and was a "borderline toxic leader."
* She created an environment in which "people are afraid of her."[10]

---

10 "Investigation: Commander Tried to Fudge Her Tape Test," *Army Times*, July 8, 2015, accessed April 24, 2016, https://www.armytimes.com/story/military/2015/07/08/glenda-lock-fired-mcdonald-army-health-center-investigatoin/29871027/.

I don't know if any of the allegations against Colonel Lock are true, nor will I assume they're not true just because she's black, but after reading many articles about the investigation, coupled with my own experiences and the experiences of other black professionals, I had to wonder how many times Colonel Lock had been verbally attacked by her staff. How often was Colonel Lock made to feel she was inferior to her peers and, as a result, shown less respect? Did Colonel Lock feel a sense of belonging or isolation in the workplace? Did Colonel Lock feel she was a part of the *workplace family*? Was Colonel Lock just as afraid of her staff as they claimed to have been of her, and was creating what they said was an authoritarian climate the result of Colonel Lock's having to walk into a hostile work environment every day and having to lead people who did not prefer to be led by a person with her skin color?

Although the investigation concluded with the army finding Colonel Lock not guilty of any criminal or ethical wrongdoing related to the tape process, the military relieved her of duty because of a poor command climate— one that many people said had predated her arrival.

As I stated earlier, for black professionals, only two facts seem to matter:

* Fact #1: We are black and therefore are more likely to be the antagonists and aggressors.

* Fact #2: Our accusers are not black and are therefore assumed to be the helpless victims.

The stories of alleged black tyranny are endless, but here's another story about the intrinsic fear many have of black leaders. One afternoon while I was eating lunch outside, an elderly black man walked up to me and asked if I had heard the good news. I said that I hadn't, but I could tell by the excited look on his face that he was about to tell me. He said, "The company just announced that it's selected a black man for the CTO [chief technical officer] position, which makes him the first and only black person hired into the executive ranks." The exciting news made me forget about my half-eaten lunch and for the next ten minutes, two complete strangers bonded over the accomplishments of one of our own.

Surprised that I hadn't heard the good news prior to this encounter, once I was back at my office, I searched online hoping to find a bio so that I could learn more about the newly appointed CTO. I couldn't find the bio, but I found a website discussion forum containing anonymous posts from former employees and former peers excoriating the newly minted CTO both professionally and personally. People questioned his suitability for the job, his knowledge of the job, his leadership acumen for the job, and—as was only fitting for a black leader—his temperament for the job. People also questioned his education and one poster commented on the physical weight of his wife. The black tyrant total grew by one.

My professional journey has been the same as that of many other black professionals. As a result, the mental and emotional preparations required to withstand the criticism, verbal attacks, and hostility that often come with entry into a new leadership position overshadow the excitement of a new job. These attacks have run the gamut from personal attacks against me to attacks against my wife. The venomous words that members of my staff have said to me are words they would never utter to a nonblack boss. How do I know this? Because many staff members have proclaimed that I brought out the worst in them; I made them do and say things they'd never done or said before. Perhaps what they were really trying to say was that my black skin brought out the worst in them.

I stopped sharing these attacks with my boss to avoid the labeling that I am a hypersensitive and ineffective leader incapable of doing my job. I also find it exhausting and insulting to have to convince my boss that I am not the cause of such unprofessional behavior. In the boss's eyes, my staff must have had legitimate reasons to treat me so poorly. There is: my black skin.

Within weeks, and sometimes days of my arrival, the workplace attacks often start with questions about how I acquired the position, because selecting me over the other interviewed applicants surprises many people. I am often asked who do I know in the company who might have given me an advantage over the other interviewed applicants? What unique sets of skills or experiences I might possess that would separate me from the other interviewed applicants. The fact that a black person may have been the most qualified applicant is outside the realm of possibility to many, so the questioning continues hoping to uncover a more plausible explanation. I often encounter at least one staff member who feel compelled to tell me that I only received the position because he or she turned the position down. This may well be true, but is this something you'd tell your new boss when you first meet him? You might—if the boss is black.

I remember starting a new job and holding my first staff meeting to formally introduce myself and to find out more about each member of the team. After I provided a few brief details about my education and background and learning more about who they were, I opened the floor for questions. The first question was about my familiarity with a specific process-improvement model. Although I was intimately familiar with the model, I framed my response around the message of teamwork. I expressed my eagerness to combine their knowledge and understanding of the model with my own, and together we would use the model for the good of the company. I wanted to pull those words back the moment they left my lips. The look of disappointment on the faces of some of the people who stared back at me was horrifying and—to be honest—somewhat intimidating, and I do not intimidate easily. At that moment, I lost all credibility, which I suspect wasn't much.

Many of them were looking for one reason to discredit my existence and withhold their respect, and my failure to provide an absolute and definitive response was it. A pattern of rudeness and disrespect began after that meeting. One staff member regularly reminded me that I was a mediocre manager and an ineffective leader. He would also tell me that his staff (he was one of the supervisors in my charge) didn't respect me, and neither did he. I swear this person must have set a recurring reminder in his Microsoft Outlook to insult me, because I could set my watch to his regular reminders of my shortcomings and inadequacies. He often told me that I'm not respected the same as my peers—they were both nonblack. During performance feedback sessions he would tell me that he didn't care about my evaluation of him because my opinions of him didn't matter.

I've had staff members refuse to face me during one-on-one meetings. The most bizarre case was a staff member who, during one such a meeting, kept his arms tightly folded while sternly looking away. Even when it was his turn to speak, his arms remained folded, and he continued to look away. I didn't observe the same bizarre behavior during the one-on-one meetings he had with other members of the leadership staff who didn't share my skin color—which was no one.

I've had staff members abruptly storm out of one-on-one meetings, often cursing at me and even throwing paper at me before they did so. I've experienced it all in pro-diversity, anti-discriminatory corporate America. These examples of disrespect didn't occur only once or twice in my career; they occurred on every job in which I oversaw a staff of people. I can say from my experiences (which align with the experiences of other black professionals) that reporting to a black person is implicitly challenging for many nonblack people in the workplace. Reporting to a black person goes against everything that is believed to be normal; therefore, creating dissonance for many and underlying tension between nonblack employees and their black bosses. Workplaces across the country comprise black professionals subjected to bullying and harassment by their staff. This doesn't fit the black-tyrant narrative.

I've never experienced the same degree of disrespect from black staff members; I've never once experienced harassment. Generally, I have to address their assumption that they'll receive favoritism because we share the same skin color. I can understand why many saw me as a much-needed sigh of relief after nonblack bosses casted them aside for so long. Once I make it known that their skin color wont garner favoritism from me, a mutually respectful relationship begins—some not without challenges, but mutually respectful.

Accusing black professionals of bullying and cultivating hostile and toxic work environments is the "nuclear option" that people often use to take down black professionals in corporate America. The power behind these accusations is so simple that it's brilliant—who wouldn't believe it? Some of the people you work with know the power behind the accusation, so knowing how to protect yourself is critical. I once heard someone say, "The more you know the law, the less likely someone can use the law against you because of your ignorance." The same applies to the laws, regulations, and corporate policies that govern your workplace environment. Loose familiarity with these policies is not enough—you need to know them from top to bottom. Others are relying on your ignorance.

Only once in my career have I faced allegations by staff members of bullying and creating a hostile and toxic work environment, but that experience was one time too many. Perhaps the allegers thought I'd wilt under pressure or that I'd take a defeatist approach and simply roll over and accept the outcome; perhaps they thought I'd become frustrated and seek employment elsewhere. I did none of these things—I fought back and won!

Because I'm familiar with how to handle allegations of this nature, I knew that a requirement for substantiating evidence was that the accusers had to produce written, tangible accounts of wrongdoing. I also knew that once my boss received such accounts of wrongdoing, it was his responsibility to perform a thorough and unbiased investigation. Despite my boss's claims that he'd repeatedly asked the accusers for written accounts of wrongdoing, no one produced a single written incident. Then, since he had nothing to investigate, it was his responsibility to swiftly put the allegations to rest, both with the accusers and with me. This didn't happen (at least not right away). Instead, I walked around for months humiliated with a gray cloud of suspicion following my every move.

On the other end of the spectrum, the allegers walked around emboldened. I asked to meet with one alleger to discuss a work related matter and he said, "I don't think so." Another would scowl at me whenever possible. I'm sure many believed the end of the black tyrant-era was fast approaching, or so they'd hoped. Many were probably taking bets on who would acquire my soon-to-be-vacant office; they'd soon see their celebrations were premature.

These allegations seared into my soul and permeated every facet of my being. My wife said that she no longer recognized me because, although I was physically present, I was distant to her and to our newborn son. Everything in my life had become secondary to clearing my name; as a result, I became the embodiment of tunnel vision.

After months of feeling disregarded and confused by my boss's words and inactions, I took a huge leap of faith and reached out to his boss and another senior leader for help. I'm not sure what I hoped to receive as a response, but I knew that it was time to pursue a different course of action. My boss's boss had always advertised an open-door policy for his *workplace family*, so if ever there was a time to take him up on that offer, this was it.

Much to my disappointment, pursuing this different course didn't yield the results I'd hoped. The silence from my boss's boss and the senior leader was deafening, and the message that I was on my own became loud and clear. It takes a tremendous amount of not caring to ignore an email from a family member in distress. It's because of this and other experiences—to include the experiences of other black professionals—that I can confidently say that management's claim to see black professionals as family is sheer nonsense. My boss didn't see me as family, nor did his boss. They both saw me as a workplace threat to eliminate.

I remember my wife pulling me aside one night and, with tears in her eyes, expressing her support and decreeing that I go to the ends of the earth to clear my name using all the resources at my disposal. The next day, I withdrew $10,000 from our checking account, placed it in a duffel bag, and set my sights on finding the best employment attorney in the area. Looking back, toting a bagful of money was a little dramatic, but I was livid and not thinking clearly.

After giving my boss ample time to clear my name, and after giving his boss and others an opportunity to intervene, it was time to take matters into my own capable hands. I was seeing red by this point. I had the financial ability to launch an all-out legal assault. Once I had an attorney lined up, the wait for workplace justice began. In the meantime, I became more introverted than I already am. A hermit, if you will. I stopped opening the blinds and turning on the lights in my office, and instead, spent each day with headphones covering my ears from the moment I arrived to work until it was time to go home. Although I continued to put in an honest day's work for an honest day's pay, clearing my name remained my focus.

Once it became known that I had legal representation, I seemed to have everyone's attention—but it was too little, too late. My boss and his boss wanted the matter resolved quickly, while I wanted legal war. I wanted everyone involved to hurt like my wife was hurting. I wanted them to hurt like my newborn son must have been hurting. I wanted them to hurt like I was hurting. I wanted to take all the hurt, humiliation, and disappointment that my family and I was feeling and ram it down their throats with the force and intensity of a commercial grade concrete demolition hammer!

Once again, God's laughter must have been thunderous, because none of my wants materialized. Instead, it would take wise counsel from my attorney and an unexpected hospital admission that rendered me unable to state the current month or the name of the sitting US president for cooler heads to prevail. While lying in that hospital bed connected to wires and tubes, and various other medical devices that filled my hospital room with beeps, bells, and dings, I had an epiphany. Everyone involved had many ways to get satisfaction at my expense, and the thought of them celebrating while doctors worked tirelessly to restore 100% function to a critical organ was unacceptable. I wouldn't give them the opportunity, I decided.

Once I returned to work, I said that I was open to talks of resolution. Things moved swiftly from that point on. It took a week to put to rest the allegations and a cloud of suspicion that had followed me for months. I walked away with the best prize of all—a resolution agreement signed by my boss, my boss's boss, my attorney, and me outlining the reversal of all disciplinary actions my boss had taken against me, amongst other things. I never doubted that the bittersweet taste of victory would one day be mine to savor, and I let the taste linger for as long as possible.

This story also has a surprise ending. The $10,000 eventually made its way back into my account. Hindsight is 20/20, but it didn't take perfect hindsight vision to see that a recently hired and recently disgruntled staff member, with the active participation (or sheer predictability) of the boss's right-hand man, were the masterminds behind the plan to overthrow me—or at the very least, sully my professional reputation. This is how the plan should have worked. The recently disgruntled staff member would plant a seed in the ear of the boss's right-hand man that members of my staff feared for their lives but were too afraid to come forward. The disgruntled staff member knew that the boss's right-hand man was essential to his plan's success, so it took a great deal of confidence that he would rush this potentially tyrant-sacking information to the boss. The disgruntled staff member also knew that to keep his hands clean, conspiring with staff members beforehand would not be an option; it was therefore imperative that he carefully drop the names of one or two staff members (pawns) who, if asked, would leap at the opportunity to nail me to the wall.

The disgruntled staff member must have calculated that after the boss received an earful from the one or two carefully selected pawns, the boss wouldn't sit idle and do nothing, especially with information passed along from someone from the same industry affiliation as the boss. The disgruntled staff member must have gambled that the first action the boss would take would be to call the pawns to his office for questioning. After receiving an earful about my reign of terror, the boss's next action would be to take punitive actions against the black tyrant.

The final but critical component of the disgruntled staff member's plan was timing. He knew, because I told him, that I'd be out on a particular Friday, and therefore the plan from beginning to end had to execute on the same day of my absence so that I would be blindsided on my return to work the following Monday. Everything up to this point occurred as planned.

When I returned to work the following Monday, I received notification that on the previous Friday, the boss and his right-hand man called a few members of my staff to their offices for questioning. I also received notification that a staff member (who the boss did not call to question) provided unsolicited input, because the opportunity to take a few swipes at the black tyrant was too great to pass up; this brought the total count to four, including the disgruntled staff member. Later the same morning, I received a text message from my boss requesting that I report to his office immediately. Since nothing was unusual about receiving such a text message, I didn't hesitate to drop everything and report to his office.

When I arrived, he informed me of the multiple allegations that my staff members had made against me the previous Friday, and by whom. Without question, without reason and without allowing me to respond, my boss flat out told me that he believed that the allegations were true. My boss's face filled with emotion when he expressed concern for the wellbeing of the disgruntled staff member who'd reported that working for me made him feel physically ill. He was considering removal of this employee from my charge out of concern for the employee's health.

He concluded the conversation by explaining in detail the multiple disciplinary actions he had taken against me and his expectations of me moving forward. He presented two pre-written documents for me to sign and initial. The last sentence you read is not a typo. Prior to my boss calling me to his office, he had already taken disciplinary actions against me. The impulsive actions made by my boss transported me to a bygone era when laws stripped black people of all forms of due process. It was not a bygone era, though, but the twenty-first century. I sat stunned!

I specifically asked him why he had chosen not to perform a thorough investigation (including allowing me to respond before taking disciplinary actions), and the next words that left his mouth were telling about how he saw me. He said his actions were not disciplinary in nature, which could only mean that he saw me as someone who lacked the mental capacity to know the difference between disciplinary and nondisciplinary actions. The absurdity of his answer is that as fellow leaders, he and I had received some of the same training, including the various forms of employee disciplinary actions. Of these various forms, he had taken two against me, with a third in the works.

The decline of my health began in that office on that day. A few weeks later, and with a doctor's note in hand, I informed my boss that the ordeal had taken a toll on my health. Instead of my boss showing the same concern for me that he'd shown for the health and wellbeing of the disgruntled staff member—the one who reported that working for me made him physically ill; my boss told me I could skip two meeting appearances, but then I had to perform the job the company hired me to do.

This experience is a great example of why black professionals should always be on guard in the workplace, especially around those who try to put them at ease. The same boss a month earlier had praised me in writing on my professionalism, leadership, and team cohesiveness. On my birthday, he provided a handwritten note in which he thanked me for my friendship and counsel. This was laughable in hindsight because my boss forgot about these formerly praiseworthy qualities when the opportunity arose to join forces with a handful of his own to hoist my head and neck in the workplace noose with the only thing left to do was kick the chair from up under my feet and watch workplace consciousness slowly slip away.

The boss's right-hand man's response to his role in the matter was predictably cowardice. He was carrying out the orders of the boss. I would never sacrifice my integrity to carry out the unethical orders of my boss. Abetting a disgruntled staff member, who is also a family friend, in carrying out a witch-hunt during my absence was unethical, pure and simple. He should have followed protocol and addressed these allegations made by my staff members at the lowest level—me—before going to my boss.

He knows this; therefore, I am inclined to believe his failure to do so was by design.

As I stated previously, two facts seem to matter here:

- Fact #1: We are black and therefore are more likely to be the antagonists and aggressors.
- Fact #2: Our accusers are not black and are therefore assumed to be the helpless victims.

There is nothing more satisfying than for a nonblack boss to perpetuate the lies, negativity, and stereotypes of black professionals; therefore, when my boss announced his plans to retire, I was certain he would share with his replacement a skewed account of what took place—skewed in his favor, of course. It was incumbent on me to share with my boss's successor the facts validated by the signed resolution agreement.

On the advice of a few trusted friends, I met with my new boss within the first few weeks of his arrival. My goals were simple: (1) Introduce myself. (2) Share the facts—signed resolution agreement. (3) And express my desire to get off to a good working start. The meeting was awkward, and the response from my new boss was not what I'd hoped to receive. I was hoping to receive words of empathy for what I went through and words of reassurance that working for him would be different. Maybe even, words of support. He was apathetic. Victim-blaming best describes how I felt during the meeting based on numerous comments he made. I walked away from the meeting feeling worse than I did when I arrived. Victim blaming also best describe how I felt weeks after the meeting—again, based on numerous comments he made. My new boss and I eventually established an amiable working relationship, but it took him having to "warm up" to me. Why is a warm up period only required for black professionals? I believe he, like the previous boss, is a good person; however, that does not equate to having a genuine concern for the wellbeing of black professionals. I stand firm on my belief that showing support to or feeling empathy for black professionals doesn't come natural for many nonblack bosses, peers, staff, and coworkers alike.

CHAPTER 8

Cognitive Dissonance

* * *

According to cognitive dissonance theory, as explained on www.simplypsychology.org:

There is a tendency for individuals to seek consistency among their cognitions (i.e., beliefs, opinions). When there is an inconsistency between attitudes or behaviors (dissonance), something must change to eliminate the dissonance. Dissonance can be reduced in one of three ways.

First, individuals can change one or more of the attitudes, behavior, beliefs…so as to make the relationship between the two elements a consonant one.

A second (cognitive) method of reducing dissonance is to acquire new information that outweighs the dissonant beliefs.

A third way to reduce dissonance is to reduce the importance of the cognitions (i.e., beliefs, attitudes).[11]

---

11 Saul McLeod, "Cognitive Dissonance," simplypsychology.org, 2008, last modified 2014, accessed October 16, 2016, http://www.simplypsychology.org/cognitive-dissonance.html.

Have you ever wondered why old photos of a black person hanging from a tree or other horrific acts inflicted on black people often included bystanders smiling proudly for the camera? Why in these photos did no one ever appear disturbed, uncomfortable, or squeamish by acts that would disturb most people? One evening while I was picking up my toddler son, I witnessed a child on the floor having an uncontrollable seizure; the memory still disturbs me many months later. Yet the people in these photos could smile proudly for the photographer while standing within a few feet of the aftermath of horrific acts. This is beyond appalling.

Who in his or her right frame of mind could smile while standing underneath a swinging corpse or while standing within a few feet of a still-smoldering body that had been burned alive? No one, because doing so would be barbaric and counter to everything that is normal. Using the cognitive dissonance theory, the people in these photos could smile because they had resolved the inconsistency in their cognition by acquiring new information to resolve the dissonance. Because the smiling people in these photos didn't consider the object swinging from the tree or the charred and smoldering object as human, these horrific acts caused no dissonance and didn't conflict with their cognition. History also tells us that onlookers often took home charred body parts such as tongues, livers, hearts, and testicles as lasting souvenirs of these events. Talk about a lack of dissonance!

Continuing with the cognitive-dissonance theme, those who were directly or indirectly involved in the plan to take me down are all married with kids. They know the importance of providing for one's family. Yet no one gave a damn about the effects that the allegations may have on my career, my livelihood, and my ability to support and provide for my wife and newborn son. Like the people smiling in those horrific photos, these people were beaming with excitement over the possibility of professionally lynching or burning my career. They resolved their dissonance by telling themselves that whatever happened to me was not because of what they'd done to me but because of what I'd done to myself; their cognition thus remained intact.

I wish the illogical reasoning stopped there. I'm still talking about me, the black tyrant, so it doesn't. The sheer arrogance from many of those who were involved speaks to a level of privilege that I and other black professionals will never experience or understand. Instead of the unknowing pawns being angry with the disgruntled staff member who used them in his poorly executed plan, they were angry with me. It was somehow my fault that they had prematurely popped champagne bottles. It was somehow my fault that they couldn't produce a single account of wrongdoing despite having ample time to do so. It was somehow my fault for fighting like hell to get the professional noose from around my neck. Many of them expected that their sheer dislike and disdain for me would be enough to remove me from my position; when that didn't happen, they were livid—at me. Not once in my career did I think that my dislike for my boss—and I've had many unlikable bosses—would be enough to justify his or her termination or reassignment. Yet, these people thought without any substantiated accounts of wrongdoing, their dislike for me would suffice for my removal. Their sheer arrogance and privilege I will never in my lifetime experience or understand.

After emerging victoriously from these allegations, some of the same people that months earlier were hoisting my head and neck into the workplace noose were showering me with compliments about my professionalism and leadership skills, and some even expressed their fondness for working for me. I guess if you can't beat 'em, join 'em. A staff member once accused me of having a chip on my shoulder, and what I wanted to say was, "You're damn right; you would, too, if you had to walk into a hostile work environment every day and deal with people like you." Instead, I kept my mouth shut and offered a big Cheshire Cat smile.

CHAPTER 9

No Respect

* * *

I'S EASIER TO THREAD A camel through the eye of a needle than for black people to receive the same level of respect in the workplace as their peers.

After analyzing the stories of the many black professionals I interviewed for this book, along with my own stories, I've concluded that the frustrations and challenges black professionals face in corporate America are due to a lack of respect. A lack of respect manifests themselves in the workplace in many ways, as I'll show in the following examples.

After I've assigned a task to a staff member, the task recipient often asks me whether the task is coming from me or from my boss. I've answered this question enough times to know that my staff members consider tasks from my boss to be relevant and reasonable, while tasks from me are irrelevant and a waste of their time and effort.

One day my creative side got the best of me, so I devised an experiment to determine if I could benefit from my staff's lack of respect for me. I quickly established the conditions. I would say that time-sensitive tasks came from the boss, while tasks with relaxed deadlines were from me. I found that even if the task were ambiguous or the deadline were unreasonable, staff members would hand in high-quality and on-time work if they thought the task came from the boss. Even previously assigned tasks from me that resulted in the gnashing of teeth now received an open-arm welcome after I'd repackaged the task as having come from the boss. The experiment worked flawlessly. Many years later, staff members still occasionally ask me about the origin of tasks, but I no longer hide behind the authority of my boss. Instead, I say the task came from me and then brace myself to be harassed.

My complimentary emails to my staff to say thanks, well done, or congratulations usually go unanswered. Weighed on its own, this doesn't mean much, because such complimentary emails generally don't warrant a response. But when compared to the responses like "No problem!", "Glad I could help!", or "Anytime!" that my staff sends in response to complimentary emails from nonblack peers and other leaders, it speaks volumes. Perhaps it's difficult to show appreciation for a compliment given by someone who's seen as intellectually inferior, unqualified to hold the position, and a frightening, threatening, and intimidating bully.

The only way for me to remain informed about matters that involve my staff is to request to be included on all email correspondence that they send to leaders at my level and above. I don't prefer to make such requests, since this border on micromanagement, and I try hard to avoid that. At every job I've had, though, I've worked with staff members whose actions suggest that their goal is to push me as far away as possible and keep me in the dark on all matters. As a result, it's a common occurrence for my peers and others to know more about the successes, challenges, and overall undertakings of my staff than I do. I remain in the dark on most things resulting in one blindside encounter after another. I believe these actions are deliberate to sabotage a boss whom they do not respect personally or professionally. Even with a requirement for email inclusion in place, I've yet to receive 100 percent adherence on any job

Peers and senior leaders who often collude with my staff to undermine my authority. One staff member said in response to my request to be included on all email correspondence, "Every time I include you on emails, [specific name of senior leader] takes you off." It's not surprising that I've yet to receive 100% adherence.

It never gets old to see others in the workplace sidestep my authority by tasking my staff directly, knowing the staff member probably won't bring these tasks to my awareness. I tend to stay in the dark on how my personnel resources are used. My boss or a peer will seek direction and guidance from one of my staff members on matters that he or she should know to address at my level. I'm left to wonder how many decisions my staff have made that were unknown to me.

It has always been a requirement that I advance-approve all non-health-related schedule changes, such as early departure, overtime, or time off. This is not that unusual a request; my boss expects the same of me. When I'm seeking my boss's approval, however, I don't tell the boss what work-schedule changes I'll be making but rather what changes I'd like to make, with the boss's approval. If only my staff would show me the same level of respect. At least one staff member—usually more—never seems to grasp asking for my approval. Instead, they tell me of any schedule modifications, sometimes after the fact. It's also common for staff members to tell me that a more senior leader approved their work-schedule modification or knows of their work-schedule modification, as if that makes usurping my authority OK. Sometimes I'm so exhausted from my blackness that all I can say is, "Sure, OK."

If your workplace follows customs or norms such as saying sir and ma'am, mister and miss, or standing to respectfully acknowledge specific levels of leadership, then keep an eye out for the frequently loose adherence or disregard altogether for black leaders. A common occurrence for me while in the presence of a staff member and a nonblack peer is that the staff member will address me by first name but will address my nonblack peer as Mr. or Ms., followed by his or her last name.

Sometimes the lack of respect is so subtle that it's hard to recognize it while it's happening. Observe how those in the workplace treat your office and how they treat the offices of those who do not share your skin color. For starters, the assumption is that you're never busy, so barging in is a common occurrence for the offices of many black professionals, while those who do not share your skin color receive the courtesy of being asked, "Are you busy" or "Do you have a moment?" Notice also how in your office, visitors will often move your furniture and other trinkets or even rudely put their feet up on your furniture—actions you will not observe them doing in the offices of those who do not share your skin color.

Other personal examples of lack of respect include exclusion from important emails, conference calls, or meetings; being passed over for introductions when distinguished visitors are present; and staff members going over my head when they hope to get different guidance because they don't like the guidance I've given them. I can't forget about senior leaders who secretly push the agenda and desires of my staff members instead of encouraging the staff member to allow me to address their concerns.

I haven't witnessed this same lack of respect for nonblack leaders, even for those who deserved it. Everywhere

I've worked has had leaders who yelled and berated co-workers and yet remain highly respected and regarded in the company. Even when these fixtures go off the professional rails—and I've witnessed this happen many times, and I've also been on the receiving end of their unprofessional tirades—their halos never seem to diminish.

Respect for nonblack leaders is immediate, and it takes unprofessional behavior of epic proportions for respect to be lost. Behavior that would send the already low respect meter of a black leader plummeting doesn't affect our nonblack counterparts. Benefit of the doubt can only explain why these nonblack leaders receive respect at the onset of their employment. The immediate assumption is that they have a solid education, relevant experience and qualifications, and belongingness—the right to be there. In contrast, the earning of respect is only a requirement for black professionals. The immediate assumptions of blacks are not as positive, which results in a wait-and-see approach: How long will it take to confirm that the pre-conceived assumptions and biases are true? This explains why your boss has to warm up to you, and no one else.

Be suspicious of your boss, peers, staff, or coworkers who claim that they've lost respect for you, because to lose something implies that someone once had it. Respect and treatment go hand in hand. Based on the treatment of black professionals in corporate America, no one respects them, so there's no respect to lose. I've had a few embolden staff members who jumped at the opportunity to share with me why they didn't respect me, usually citing incidents in which I'd said or done something that, of course, made them *feel uncomfortable*. Their words went in one ear and immediately out the other. I've witnessed nonblack leaders scold, berate, and embarrass these same staff members, but these nonblack leaders never suffer degradation on the respect meter. The behavior of these nonblack leaders is justified by, "Oh that's just how he is."

Does any of what you've read so far in this book sound like the corporate experiences of someone respected in the workplace? When members of my staff interrogate me within days or weeks of my arrival because they're in disbelief someone selected me for the job, is that respect? When staff members conspire against me with allegations that even they can't substantiate, is that respect? When my boss shows immediate warmth to my peers but treat me as if I'm a ticking time bomb, is that respect? When someone in the workplace tapes my name and the word "nigger" to the walls, is that respect?

CHAPTER 10

ABM/ABW

* * *

If we are upset, we are angry!
If we are sarcastic, we are angry!
If we are opinionated, we are angry!
If we are stern, we are angry!
If we are overly inquisitive, we are angry!
If we disagree, we are angry!
If our voice becomes a pitch higher, we are angry!

IT'S IMPOSSIBLE FOR MANY BLACK professionals to escape
the workplace labels angry black man (ABM) or angry
black woman (ABW). It doesn't matter who you are, how
important you may think you are, or how important you
may think others think you are; many people in the workplace will believe that you're one disagreement away from
a violent outburst. Your boss, peers, staff, and coworkers
treat you the same way they'd treat finding a suspicious
package with wires sticking out of the side: very delicately.

When in your presence they walk on eggshells out of fear that, like the suspicious package, you will explode!

Disruptive outbursts in meetings, the slamming of doors and other objects, and bouts of uncontrollable verbal abuse by our nonblack counterparts are all the result of their passion, drive, and pursuit of excellence. I'll never forget the time I overheard a handful of people outside my office engaging in one-upmanship over who'd had the most harrowing encounter with a particular workplace leader. Despite each story sounding more hostile than the last, despite each story sounding more unprofessional than the last, and despite each story sounding more verbally abusive and toxic than the last, some of the words never mentioned were *angry, threatening, hostile,* or *bully.* Their stories sounded to me like they were describing unprofessional behavior, but I could tell by the sprinkled-in words of praise and reverence that these stories were an endearing walk down memory lane for this particular leader.

I remember witnessing an incident in which a nonblack member of the senior leadership staff verbally ripped a nonblack employee to shreds. If words, tone, facial expression, and body language were bullets, then the employee on the receiving end of the verbal assault would have been Swiss cheese. The climax of the conversation was instantaneous: a question the employee asked resulted in the senior leader attacking with fully deployed claws. The actions of the senior leader wouldn't surprise most people, because for years people justified his volatile behavior with the often-used excuse, "That's just how he is." On this day, he was in rare form.

I pride myself on having thick and somewhat impenetrable skin, but the longer I stood watching, the more uncomfortable I became as I witnessed the verbal assault that was unfolding right in front of me. The incident didn't sit well with me; apparently, the incident also didn't sit well with a handful of onlookers, who stopped by my office to complain about witnessing the verbal assault of one of my staff members. I allowed a few days to pass before pulling the victim into my office so that I could apologize on behalf of his attacker. After he took a moment to recall the incident, my apology seems to have caught him off guard, since he didn't find the behavior of this leader rude or offensive.

I was speechless because had I or another black professional engaged in behavior that was half as severe, this employee and every onlooker would have petitioned for my immediate removal. How do I know this? I know this because a slight elevation of my voice or a subtle wrinkle in my forehead is enough to send my boss, peers, staff, and coworkers running for cover, but the verbal assault by this senior leader who didn't share my skin color was no big deal.

Since there's no way to escape being labeled an ABM or ABW, as black professionals, we confirm the assumptions and biases of others when we avoid making eye contact, speak only when spoken to, or fail to practice common courtesies such as saying hello, please, and thank you. Is there really a need for many of us to remain in the frowning-and-standoffish mode? I get it. The workplace can be frustrating and even hostile to black professionals, and smiling doesn't come easy most days. While others can show up to work and just be themselves, we have to be "on", "guarded", and "un" at all times: un-intimidating, un-threatening, un-angry, and un-black. Relaxing at work is not a luxury we can afford. But black professionals shouldn't hand their bosses, peers, or coworkers confirmation of their assumptions and biases against them on a silver platter. Be unapologetically black but also be smart.

Black women, I've passed many of you in the halls or sat across from you in meetings, and the frown you often display can be a natural repellent, even for me. I get it, but you have to do better. Considering how challenging the workplace can be for a black man, it must be twice as challenging for you, being black and a woman. Not only do you have to deal with the same nonsense as black men, but you also have to deal with feelings of never measuring up to society's idea of workplace beauty and presence, which sometimes causes you to compromise your authentic self just to fit in. For example, you can't change your hairstyle without considering the reactions of your boss and coworkers. Are braids too ethnic? Is an afro too militant? It saddens me that black people like me can't openly express black culture in the workplace lest we face accusations of being against everything else.

A great example of black women never measuring up to society's description of beauty and presence in the workplace occurred after Barack Obama's election as US president. Several nonblack coworkers outwardly expressed their opinions of how unattractive they found Michelle Obama. Not only was she unattractive, many of them said, but she also lacked sophistication and therefore was an embarrassment to the country. While I listened to their criticism, I wondered if they realized or cared that when I see Michelle Obama, I see my mom, my sisters, my aunts, and my wife. I've never met Michelle Obama, but I have no doubt that she is a beautiful black woman both inside and out. Was it a coincidence that the election of Barack Obama as US President was the first time I'd heard the attractiveness and sophistication of the first lady called into question?

Black men and women, it's only natural that at some point you'll become angry in the workplace, but unlike your nonblack counterparts—in which others judge their displays of anger on an incident-by-incident basis—you shouldn't expect any passes from your boss, peers, staff, or coworkers for momentarily losing your cool. Instead, all it takes is one display of anger to earn a shiny and permanent ABM or ABW label.

By the way, the words *assertive* and *angry* are close cousins. The only time black professionals can be assertive in the workplace without accusations of black tyranny is when they're dealing with workplace castaways who have proven useless or difficult to deal with elsewhere, so off to the ABM or ABW camp they go for some much-needed tough and angry love. A black person can hit these castaways over the head every morning and afternoon with a rubber mallet and no one will care. These misfits are lost causes. It isn't easy for nonblack professionals to become lost causes, so you know they must be beyond rehabilitation.

CHAPTER 11

Problems? What Problems?

* * *

Wʜᴇɴ ʙʟᴀᴄᴋ ᴘʀᴏꜰᴇssɪᴏɴᴀʟs ʜᴀᴠᴇ ᴘʀᴏʙʟᴇᴍs in the work-place, they're often told that they have to get over it. Many black professionals, throughout their careers, find them-selves getting over "it" more than getting "it" resolved. Damn you, "it"!

One of the most bizarre workplace experiences I've had occurred shortly after I accepted a job as a senior network engineer. My job started on the same day as a nonblack employee name "Billy". Billy and I became fast friends after discovering that we had several things in common. He'd started his career as a software engineer before finding his niche in network engineering; he was an "IT certification whore," a name that describes some-one who gains IT certifications for the sake of gaining IT certifications; and he was an overachiever for honing his network-engineering skills.

The biggest difference between Billy and me was his shaky confidence because of his limited experience in the network-engineering field. It seemed like yesterday when I had been the junior engineer, so I could empathize with how he was feeling. In many ways he reminded me of myself, so I offered him something that no one had ever offered me: a technical and professional mentor. It wouldn't take long for me to realize that it was me who needed the support, not Billy.

The first indicator that something was awry was the seating assignments. Billy received all the accoutrements one would expect when starting a new job: desk, chair, phone, PC, and shortly after arrival, email and network-equipment login accounts. All I received was a large wooden ethernet cable spool to sit on, which was uncomfortable, so I spent most of my days standing. Besides not having the most basic workplace amenities to start my job, I didn't have email or network-equipment login accounts.

One afternoon I came across Billy discussing the contents of a large network diagram that one of the senior engineers was holding. Eager to get in on the discussion and (I hoped) engineering action, I positioned myself to see and hear what they were discussing. While I was standing there, I constantly adjusted my position to maintain a good view of the network map, since it kept moving outside my view. It took a few moments before realizing that this seemed to be because of the deliberate actions of the map holder. After ten minutes of playing "now you see it, now you don't," I finally got the message that my presence was not welcome, and I left to tidy up the network-test lab—non-brain-cell-requiring stuff.

A few hours later, Billy found me and apologized for what he described as an awkward and uncomfortable moment. I was just relieved that someone other than me had noticed the bizarre behavior. I contacted my boss (who worked at the corporate office a few miles away) to share my observations and he assured me that there was no need to fret.

The awkward moments continued. On many afternoons around lunchtime, Billy and most of the members of the engineering staff would go missing, leaving me alone with an uncomfortable wooden spool and millions of dollars' worth of network equipment that I couldn't log into without login accounts, which I still had yet to receive. One afternoon, while I was outside making a phone call (because employees couldn't have cell phones inside the building), I was surprised to see Billy and a carful of engineers pulling up in the same vehicle. As they walked toward me, I asked, "Where were you guys?" With as much sarcasm as he could muster, one engineer replied, "Where we were at." Billy, without acknowledging the question, or me walked into the building.

As expected, Billy came along a few hours later to offer another apology for what he described as engineers giving me the ice treatment. Billy, hoping to make sense of it all, asked if I'd known any of the engineers prior to accepting the job; this would have made sense if I had, but I hadn't. Billy also informed me that he wanted to distance himself from me, because remaining friends with me was too much of a liability. This was not the way I would have handled someone who'd offered me his mentorship and support, but I respected his decision

Several months into the new position, I was still waiting for basic office amenities. In contrast, Billy had settled in. He now had family photos and school memorabilia covering his desk and had become the go-to person for minor network issues. His confidence was increasing by the week, while my frustration was increasing by the day.

One late afternoon, several routers failed, which caused the network-monitoring screens to illuminate with brightly glowing red icons. I capitalized on the moment by asking to work the network outage. One of the senior engineers agreed, logged into the network equipment using his credentials, and stepped aside for me to take over. All the engineers stood behind me watching with their microscopes set to the highest power. I politely turned to the engineer standing closest to me and asked about the routing protocol that was used. In response, he yelled, "You tell me! You're the fucking OSPF network-engineering guru!" (This refers to the "open shortest path first" protocol.) He ushered me aside and motioned for Billy to take over, because my asking a question could only mean that I didn't know what I was doing.

The final straw occurred one morning after I arrived at work and found my name and NIGGER written on pieces of paper and taped to the walls throughout the work area. Half the people in the room appeared to be in shock over the emboldened person or people responsible for the insensitive acts, while the other half appeared terrified of my assumed reaction. What must have surprised many of them was that I was not fuming mad, mainly because this incident was just another low moment among many low moments I'd suffered since my arrival. I reported the incident to my boss, who gave me empty lip service.

The next morning when I arrived at work, I was excited to find a sticky note on my desk (I mean, wooden spool) with a message to call the corporate office, which I could only assume meant that they wanted to discuss all that I had reported. The person on the other end requested that I report to the corporate office ASAP. When I arrived at the corporate office, someone whom I had never met before led me into a conference room and pointed to an empty seat. Following a brief exchange of pleasantries, the next words I heard were, "I received a request to remove you from the contract." I sat motionless, speechless, and in total disbelief that my reward for being patient and tolerant was removal from the contract. An overwhelming sense of foolishness also came over me. It was foolish of me to believe that my boss had been working to resolve my workplace problems, since at that moment I knew that all he was working to resolve was me. To top it off, he was too cowardly to deliver the message himself.

It was protocol for the defense contractor to keep me on payroll for two weeks while the contractor secured another contract for my placement. Once the two weeks had expired, the company would enforce my termination. I didn't want to continue working for the same company, so I used the two weeks to search for external employment opportunities.

Two weeks had almost run its course when I received a notification from the defense contractor that the White House Communications Agency (WHCA) wanted to meet with me. The defense contractor was doubtful that I could close the deal because of WHCA's selective hiring practices. Moments before the interview, the defense contractor told me that the agency didn't want just anyone interfacing with White House staff; they were looking for the best of the best. The contractor's doubt that I'd receive an offer became my motivation to land a job that I really didn't want.

As expected, WHCA offered me the position on the spot, along with a litany of benefits and perks. Fortunately for me, and unfortunately for the defense contractor (which could no longer bill my network engineering services at an exorbitant rate), I landed an external opportunity and submitted my resignation.

This story doesn't end without a splash of humor. Several weeks later, I received a phone call from the defense contractor's HR department. They wanted to know the reason for my resignation. Bye!

CHAPTER 12

It's Never about You

* * *

HIRING YOU WAS NOT ENOUGH. Now you expect fairness, mentoring, and grooming?

Not once in my career have I seen a black person taken under the proverbial wing of a nonblack person for mentoring and grooming, nor have I experienced it. This has perplexed me over the years, and I've yet to arrive at a plausible explanation for why passing over black professionals is the norm, while a web of support often surrounds our nonblack counterparts. If all attributes are equal except for skin color, it's my belief that a boss selecting a black person for mentoring and professional grooming over someone who favors his or her daughter, son, niece, nephew, sister or brother would rarely, if ever occur. Similarly, the likelihood of the fast-rising fixture selecting a black person to join his or her project or collaboration team is just as rare. They want nothing to do with the black professional others ignore; the black professional doing low complexity or miniscule work; the black professional who makes him or her feel uncomfortable; or the black professional of simple acquaintance or familiarity? I've talked to countless black professionals in both the public and private sectors, and they all have the same question: What about me?

A boss showing a genuine interest in a black professional, either personally or professionally is rare. Instead, we sit idle and watch as our bosses show warmth and empathy to our nonblack peers and coworkers, resulting in avenues of support that don't include us. As one black professional told me, "My boss often stops by my work area, pulls up a chair, and chats with my nonblack cubicle mates without ever acknowledging me or even including me in their non-work-related discussions."

Another black professional shared with me that in the five years of being on a team, her boss had never recognized her; instead, she'd stood on the sidelines and watched as her nonblack teammates received recognition and awards—some, multiple times. She sought my advice about how best to broach the subject with her boss, so I suggested that she share with her boss exactly what she'd shared with me. I also advised her not to leave the discussion with her boss without seeking areas where she could improve.

A few days later, she followed up with me to inform me that her boss had seemingly been unaware that she hadn't received recognition during her five years on the team; as for areas of improvement, he had nothing to offer. Add another invisible black professional to the ranks of corporate America.

Once black professionals are introduced to the team and—if they're lucky—shown the men's and women's restrooms, they're on their own. I've had the most basic information kept from me on a few occasions. One time, when I started a new job, my boss and peers watched as I attended a weekly director-led staff meeting for over a month before they made me aware of the requirement to provide an update on the status of my team at these meetings. The reason for not telling me sooner was that "We thought you knew."

While few people see black professionals as worthwhile investments, when our nonblack counterparts arrive, they often receive all the trappings of success. Before they've outfitted their desks with vacation trinkets and family photos, their offices or workspaces have already become revolving doors of visitors stopping by to introduce themselves and welcome the up-and-coming fixtures to the team. The visits continue as others introduce the up-and-coming fixtures to other fixtures, offer assistance and guidance, or pass along valuable pieces of information about the workplace culture. Over time, these visitors become familiar faces as they pass my office or workspace without so much as a hello. The frequent desk visits eventually become lunch outings, and before you know it, a network of support has taken shape in plain sight. In no time at all, the newly minted fixtures skyrocket up the corporate ladder, thus becoming the measuring stick for every ignored black professional to achieve.

Here's a great example. I remember accepting a job as a network engineer and starting on the same day as a non-black person name "Josh". After attending new-employee orientation, we were assigned to be teammates at the Network Operations Center (NOC). The only difference between our backgrounds was that Josh had a high school diploma, while I had a bachelor of science degree and was working toward a master's degree.

It seemed from day one that success was Josh's destiny, and it didn't take long for our paths to diverge. From the moment we arrived, a web of support swarmed Josh's desk like bees to honey, while I and other black professionals watched in envy from the sidelines. Within weeks, his calendar was full of meeting invites, and his workplace social circle was growing at a steady rate. I and other black professionals received only the crumbs that accidentally dropped from the table, which were the crumbs Josh brought back to share with the rest of us. I was less than satisfied with this arrangement, because I was hungry.

I refused to sit back and watch Josh receive all the workplace spoils, so I devised a plan that would put me in the spotlight. I approached all the senior network engineers and offered to take on their most hated and mundane tasks. All I asked in return was the minimum training required to perform the job. All but one engineer happily offloaded their weeks of 4:00 a.m. rotational network-maintenance duties, and I instantly became sleep deprived. I found the work so rewarding and fulfilling that I asked for more. I was learning a lot and had placed myself in the spotlight, which led to me picking up the remaining network-maintenance work and any other grunt work the engineers threw at me.

In no time at all, I was performing tasks that were far more advanced than might be expected of someone who had my level of experience and I was accumulating a long list of accomplishments to show for it. Despite the initiative I displayed in seeking more tasks and despite my sacrifices and lack of sleep, no one seemed to notice either me or my list of accomplishments. Josh had received several awards, while I had yet to receive one. He'd been recognized numerous times; I had not. It was time to implement plan B: invest in myself outside of work.

I purchased thousands of dollars' worth of network equipment and built a CCIE-worthy network lab in my basement. (That stands for "Cisco Certified Internetwork Expert.") I purchased Cisco, Foundry, and various other pieces of network equipment, such as VPNs (virtual private networks) and firewalls, along with books, computer-based training, and online training courses. I spent many nights and weekends as a prisoner in my basement while I honed my network-engineering skills. Unfortunately, despite my best efforts at home, I remained invisible at work.

I grew to resent Josh and had reason to believe the resentment was mutual. We couldn't hide our dislike for each other; everyone in the workplace felt the tension. We wouldn't sit next to each other in meetings, and we avoided speaking to each other unless necessary. I eventually resigned, but not before the two of us sat down to bury the hatchet. It was much-needed closure to admit how I'd felt about him over the years. I asked for his forgiveness for allowing my blackness to make him feel guilty for his nonblackness. I knew all along that Josh wasn't to blame: all he did was show up to work, and the support came to him. Josh accepted my apology and surprised me by offering the same. I accepted.

This may have been my first uneven-playing-field experience, but I didn't know at the time that many more would follow. At every stop in my career, I watched as nonblack employees became fixtures while I and others who share my skin color remained accessories. The only difference between how I feel now versus how I felt when I was fresh from college is that I now accept that the workplace environment is not color-blind, I accept that the workplace environment will never be fair to black professionals, and I accept that sometimes my skin will mean the difference between success and failure. Show me any workplace in the United States of America, and I'll show you black, threatening, and invisible professionals who are desperate for recognition and inclusion.

And Then There Was One

* * *

ONLY ONE BOSS STOOD OUT from the rest during my professional journey. His name, as my wife respectfully calls him, is Colonel G.

Before I wrote a single word of this chapter, I took two weeks to reflect on the reasons I consider Colonel G to be a unique boss. His uniqueness was not in the negative sense; he was unique because he was unlike any of the numerous other bosses I encountered during my journey in corporate America. It's easy to analyze, dissect, and write about the frustrations and challenges I encountered while I worked for bosses who had no regard for me or didn't even seem to see me, but it's far more difficult to write about the intangibles that made working for Colonel G different. I'd never contemplated these differences until writing this chapter. So there I sat, two weeks later, fingers to keyboard, struggling to identify and capture what made working for Colonel G so unique.

Let's start with the first memorable encounter between us. During the interview, Colonel G asked me, "If you're selected for the position, what would be your immediate focus?"

I replied, "If I'm selected for the position, my immediate focus would be to address the workplace issues that keep you up at night." Queue the homerun music, because I'd just hit a fastball out of the park with that answer. Well, at least that's what I thought until I heard his reply. He said, "Nothing from work keeps me up at night." Based on his response, I'd clearly misjudged the trajectory and velocity of the ball, because instead of going over the fence, it was a foul ball. I thought about my response to the interview question as I sensed the job quickly slipping through my fingertips.

Later that evening, I rehashed the encounter with this arrogant-seeming man to my wife, who offered me a different perspective. She interpreted Colonel G's response as his way of making it known that he didn't allow work to bleed into his home life. His answer impressed her.

Several months later, I received an offer from him; despite receiving three other higher-level and higher-salary job offers, I accepted. Any trepidation I felt about my acceptance of the job offer vanished the moment I keyed into my new office and found the following note on my keyboard. After reading it, there was no doubt in my mind that working for Colonel G would be a unique experience.

WELCOME ABOARD!

WE ARE EXTREMELY EXCITED TO HAVE YOU JOINING OUR TEAM!

YOU HAVE A PHENOMENAL GROUP OF PROFESSIONALS WORKING FOR YOU...YOU WILL NEED TO LEVERAGE THEIR INDIVIDUAL STRENGTHS TO MAKE ALL OF "THIS WORK." I HAVE HIGH EXPECTATIONS FOR YOU, AND WILL PUSH YOU AND YOUR TEAM TO MOVE OUR PROCESSES TO THE NEXT LEVEL WHILE AT THE SAME TIME ENSURING THAT WE PROVIDE UNINTERRUPTED PRODUCTS AND SERVICES TO THE FIGHT.

SO, WELCOME ABOARD! I RECOMMEND SETTLING IN QUICK, AND STRAPPING IN FOR A GREAT RIDE!
—LT COL G

My first impressions of Colonel G were of someone who was self-assured, opinionated, intensely cerebral, and compulsively perfectionistic. He was sometimes intense and gregarious and sometimes laid-back and reserved. Many people who worked for him found these characteristics intimidating, but I welcomed them, because I share many of the same characteristics. Colonel G was a fearless leader who was not afraid to make mistakes, to admit to making mistakes, or to stand up to his superiors, sometimes to his own detriment. Colonel G expected nothing less than excellence from himself and from those who worked for him.

My first exposure to Colonel G's perfectionistic tendencies occurred after what seemed like the hundredth iteration of a PowerPoint presentation he asked me to create. The nitpicking didn't bother me, but his constant changing of what he considered "task completed" drove me nuts. My definition of "done" was his "you're not even close," but sometimes his definition of "make this last change and you're done" was "make one more change, and then you're done." My frustration grew with every change, and I finally let him know. Imagine the look on my face when he thanked me for the feedback, said that he empathized with my concerns and frustrations, and suggested that together we define the "finish line" and stick to it.

I swung the door wide open so that Colonel G could slap multiple ABM labels on me—*contentious, argumentative, angry, insubordinate, hostile,* and *threatening*—but he passed. We'd have many more passionate discussions in the years ahead, some of which caused Colonel G to smack the table or me to elevate my voice to emphasize a point, but they all ended the same way they began: with our mutual respect still intact.

Colonel G was a leader of men. This is not to imply that he was not a leader of women as well, but my tallness, dark skin, baldhead, and muscular build didn't send him shrieking to the corner, as had happened to many others in the workplace. Nor did Colonel G find my dominant personality off-putting. Instead of viewing my dominant personality as a weakness or a trait that needed suppression, he frequently expressed his desire for me to speak up more. I was shocked to have a boss encourage me to step out of the shadows and speak up. This was further evident when he'd display flashes of annoyance when he thought I was blindly following his lead or blindly agreeing with him for the sake of agreeing. He'd say, "Don't do it because of me, do it because you think it's the right thing to do." Or he'd say, "Don't agree with me for the sake of agreeing with me." Translation: he was not a yes-man, and he didn't want me to be a yes-man, either. He trusted me and he trusted my decisions.

Colonel G challenged me both professionally and personally. For example, within weeks of my arrival, he asked me to brief a high-ranking military official on a few details that I was still learning. Still very much scarred from my experiences with previous bosses, I thought that his request for me to brief this official so soon after my arrival was a deliberate setup for failure. Only a boss with a desire to commit career suicide would put a newly hired person in front of a distinguished visitor. His response to my apprehension was, "I wouldn't ask you to do it if I didn't think you were ready." He was right. I was ready.

This is just one of the many examples in which Colonel G pushed me beyond the boundaries I'd set for myself; as a result, my boundaries expanded.

Colonel G was not just a boss; he was genuinely happy at the announcement that my wife and I were expecting our first child. What meant more to me than the thoughtful gifts from the colonel and his wife were the many non-work-related conversations we had about fatherhood, parenting in general, new-dad expectations, grandparent dynamics, and much more.

When I received another job offer, it was Colonel G whom I sought to help me weigh the pros and cons. I was so fixated on the promotion and higher-salary position that I forgot about my son's anticipated birth in a few months. It was Colonel G who said, "Are you sure that creating job instability while you're on the cusp of becoming a new dad is prudent?" The answer was no. By the way, "prudent" was one of his favorite words to use.

When I encountered challenges at work and my approach was admittedly one laced with emotion instead of logic, it was Colonel G who reminded me that the actions (or inactions) of a leader speak louder than the leader's words.

Despite my high opinion of Colonel G, there were those on his staff who would disagree. The two words that others most often used to describe Colonel G were "standoffish" and "unapproachable," both of which are counter to the person I got to know. My guess is that Colonel G was not only a shock to my system but also a shock to other people's systems too. He didn't chase popularity from his staff, peers, or senior leaders, nor did he show favoritism based on race or gender. I'm not surprised that a boss and leader who treated me this fairly would draw criticism from others. He was different to me and probably just as different to them.

I've had many bosses throughout my career, some worse than others, but Colonel G—a white man—was one of a few bosses that I ever wanted to emulate and have emulated. He was a boss, mentor, and coach rolled up in one. He passed along many golden nuggets about being a better leader, but not just at work. He passed along golden nuggets about being a better father and being a better man. Colonel G started out as my boss, he became my coach and mentor, and now I consider him a friend who still takes time to provide wise counsel whenever I need it.

CHAPTER 14

CYA

* * *

THE PEOPLE YOU WORK WITH will sometimes claim to have your back, but in your time of need, they'll only show you theirs while running away from you.

To the black professionals who are reading, it's imperative that you always remain in "cover your ass" (CYA) mode. Your bosses, peers, and coworkers will smile in your face, joke with you, show warmth and sympathy, listen to your personal stories (which carelessly many black people love to divulge), and appear to be on your side. They will have you believe that they'll go to bat for you. They may even refer to you as a friend or consider you a source of counsel. They'll often steer you into a false sense of security; then, once your guard is down, they'll try to knock you flat on your ass.

The last person I considered a workplace friend turned out to be someone I didn't know at all. Despite the lunch outings and the socializing and blending of our families outside work, I later discovered that he had reached out to my boss on multiple occasions to undermine my effectiveness as a leader—and also as his boss. The irony was powerful. I'd given him a job, and now he was covertly trying to take my job away. You read about his deceptive behavior in chapters 7 and 8.

One of the hardest lessons for many black professionals to learn is that a friendly person in the workplace is often not the same as a workplace friend. Some black professionals are so starved for attention and opportunity, that they'll befriend anyone who will show them a small measure of attention and kindness. These black professionals often go to great lengths to maintain these one-sided friendships by memorizing the names of spouses and kids and memorizing important dates such as birthdays and anniversaries. Only the best gifts will do during the holidays: desserts made with grandma's secret recipe.

Never have I seen these acts of kindness reciprocated, so one would think that the black people doing the ingratiating would realize the same. Unfortunately, they often don't. While the ingratiation continues, these black professionals remain invisible with no one caring about them either personally nor professionally. It saddens me to see black professionals degrade themselves for the sake of recognition and opportunity in the midst of anti-discriminatory and diversity corporate America.

Don't expect your bosses, peers, or coworkers to relate to your issues and concerns when they struggle to relate to you. Consider the following example. You inform your boss that a nonblack person you work with was mocking a horrific scene in the movie *Twelve Years a Slave*, and despite the fact that you repeatedly told him that his comments made you uncomfortable, he continued with his mocking. Your boss, who can't relate to you but who can relate to your coworker, will assume (sometimes aloud) that the behavior you described is uncharacteristic of this coworker. With great ease, your boss labels it as "a big misunderstanding". At that moment, your boss marginalizes your concerns, and your boss's looking into the matter starts from a place of your perceived overreaction. That was a silly example, but I hope you'll get the bigger point. Sometimes it's not a big misunderstanding but rather mistreatment of and disregard for black professionals in the workplace, and that's why it's critical to know how to CYA.

To be black in America is to be paranoid and therefore, all black professionals need to master the art of CYA. There's no better tool to use than a digital recorder—but only if you live in a state that allows one-party consent recording and your workplace doesn't prohibit recording devices or recordings of any kind (which is common for the public-work sector). If you're unsure, don't do it. To reiterate what I once heard someone say, "The more you know the law, the less likely someone can use the law against you because of your ignorance." Before engaging in any recording activities read and understand—or seek legal counsel to help you understand—one-party consent and two-party consent laws and the states in which these laws apply.

Once you have cleared the legality hurdle, there's no need to run out and buy a digital recorder, since most smartphones already come equipped with recording capability; if not, as they say, "there's an app for that." Download the app, add it to your smartphone's home screen, and familiarize yourself with how to initiate recording with the least number of clicks. Sometimes you'll only have a moment's notice before you're ambushed with nonsense, and it's imperative that you capture every moment.

If people in the workplace suspect you of recording, they may opt to record you in turn, and you should let them. Others' recording of black professionals is pointless—a smartphone battery drain. The burden of proof is always on black people to prove that what we saw, heard, or experienced actually occurred. Otherwise, it didn't. Ignore the naysayers and remain focused on protecting yourself, because there are countless examples in which undisputable evidence was not enough to prove injustices against black people had occurred. Still, it's best to have solid evidence than not.

I try to live my life not saying things that I don't want repeated, so I welcome anyone who wants to record me. All I ask is to speak directly into the microphone to ensure the recording device captures my every word. Your boss, peers, staff, or coworkers won't say the same. If they ever suspect that you're recording them, they'll select their words with the precision of a skilled surgeon from fear that you may one day use their conniving, scheming, and conspiring words against them.

Now, to the black people who are reading, I know how we can take advice too far, so allow me to provide more clarity. In no way am I suggesting that you walk around your workplace with a microphone in one hand and a recording device in the other, looking for a sound bite that would make TMZ proud. Here is some perspective: only once in my professional journey did I find it a necessity to make a recording in the workplace, and that was after I'd exhausted all options for workplace justice. No one believed that my boss was spinning a false narrative, so I had to prove it.

Whenever my smartphone is close by (which is always the case), it never gets old to see the shaky knees and careful selection of words by those who knew about the one-time I recorded in the workplace.

What you're about to read next was a last-minute addition that my wife insisted I include in the book to drive home the importance of CYA. While I was commuting to work one morning in November 2016 with my toddler son in the back seat, a driver who'd dropped something in his car and had taken his eyes off the road to lean forward and pick it up, rear-ended me. The impact, although not severe enough to cause damage, created a shower of Cheerios in the backseat from a startled little boy.

I exited my vehicle to assess the damage and was thankful that none had occurred. I saw no need to prolong what was already starting out to be a crappy Monday morning, so after firmly telling the driver to keep his eyes on the road, I proceeded to get back into my vehicle when I heard a voice behind me say, "I don't like your attitude." For the next forty-five minutes, my son and I endured a series of verbal assaults and racial slurs that resulted in two calls to 911.

The driver referred to me as "big black guy", "thug", and he occasionally called me by the name of a well-known local black criminal who'd committed a series of homicides in area. According to this driver, it was obvious that I was from New York, Chicago, or Detroit—I'm not from any of those places—and he kept reminding me that he'd seen my type many times before. On multiple occasions, he attempted to provoke me into assaulting him by stepping within inches of my face. He called me a terrorist and made comments about my son, who cried in the backseat. He also made two phone calls in which he accused me of threatening him and calling him white trash.

The only bright spot that morning was that I'd captured the entire ordeal on my vehicle-dash cam; as a testament to his sheer privilege and arrogance, I made him aware on at least six occasions that recording was in session, but he didn't seem to care. I was black, he was not, end of story. Well, at least that's what he must have thought until I played portions of the recording to the police officers who arrived on the scene. Just like my ex-boss, the driver's lies had no chance against his recorded words.

Later that night, I recapped the ordeal to my wife, who cried about the fact that our toddler son and I had experienced such horrendous behavior. Fighting back tears, she reminded me that even while I wore a suit and tie with an innocent toddler in the backseat, I was nothing more than a criminal and a thug in the eyes of that man. Sadly, some of the people in the workplace see me and other black professions the same way this stranger saw me: a thug who's unworthy of respect. I can't emphasize this enough. If you're a black person and you're not comfortable using a recording device, you're a damn fool.

If you live in a state that doesn't allow recording, then email's your next best CYA choice. The number one benefit of email is nonrepudiation: the sender can't deny having sent the email, and the recipient can't deny having received the email. The cherry on top is that you capture everything in writing, as opposed to face-to-face conversations, where your word won't stand a chance against the word of a nonblack accuser. Don't misconstrue my point: face-to-face communication is always the best method for working through workplace issues. But sometimes too much emotion is involved for face-to-face communication to be effective (or safe), so email may be more appropriate.

Another benefit to using email is that some people are better communicators with written responses than with having face-to-face conversations. Despite the convenience and usefulness of email, though, one downside is capturing the right tone. To get around this, before sending an email written in an emotional state, ask someone you trust—someone who's removed from the situation—to proofread it before sending. Always stick to the facts.

As a black person you can never CYA too much. For example, I pay a monthly fee to keep a network of lawyers on retainer. I do this to ensure that in my time of legal need—whether work related or otherwise—I have access to legal advice or legal representation at a moment's notice. As long as my skin color is black, there is no limit to how far I will go to protect and defend my family and myself.

CHAPTER 15

Golden Nuggets

* * *

WHAT FOLLOWS IN THIS CHAPTER are various observations, quotes, and assertions I've amassed throughout my professional career. I refer to them as "golden nuggets" because, much like finding an actual piece of gold, I've held on to them because of their significance and value. I've broken these golden nuggets into two categories: golden nuggets for anyone and golden nuggets for black professionals.

Here are my golden nuggets for anyone. I offer the following golden nuggets as universal advice to help anyone navigate and mitigate some of the frustrations and challenges you might experience in the workplace.

* Everyone wants to improve race relations in the workplace, but no one wants to talk about it. Don't be that someone who's afraid to engage in respectful, meaningful, and constructive dialogue on race.

* Give your boss and staff (if applicable) nothing less than 100 percent.
* Don't have extraordinary expectations of ordinary people.
* In the workplace, know the difference between a friendly person and a friend.
* Do what you have to do until you can do what you want to do.
* Always have a move-up or move-on plan.
* Never compromise who you are just to fit in.
* Never settle for less, because you'll always get less than what you settled for.
* The actions of your boss, peers, and coworkers speak louder than their words.

I offer the following golden nuggets for black professionals to heighten their awareness and help mitigate some of the frustrations and challenges I've highlighted throughout this book that a black professional might face in the workplace.

* Black professionals have to work twice as hard to receive half the recognition of our nonblack counterparts.
* Whether you're a Rhodes Scholar or president of the United States, your boss, peers, staff, and coworkers implicitly believe you are intellectually

inferior. You can't convince them otherwise, so
stop trying.

* Stop viewing others in the workplace as the gold
standard that you strive to become. You will
never experience workplace freedom until you
stop caring what others think about you. Why?
Because whenever you walk into a room, the assumptions and biases that others have of you
walk in first.

* As a black professional, you have an extra responsibility to make the men and women who surround you (many of whom have no regard for your
comfort) feel comfortable at all times.

* Stop looking and listening for the smoking guns
while ignoring the loud subtleties.

* Every day on the job is a black professional's first
day on the job.

* Never assess your self-worth through the eyes of
your boss, peers, staff, or coworkers unless you
can accept "worthless" as a possible assessment.

* Job hopping is common among black professionals, but it shouldn't be. While the names, faces,
and employers may change, the overall frustrations and challenges that black professionals encounter in the workplace remain the same.

* Learning how to fight professionally is imperative
for your survival in corporate America.

- If you don't have a plan for yourself, then you'll be a part of someone else's plan; because you're black, that's no plan at all.

- Success doesn't attract others to you; it repels others from you. Don't let this stop you: never stop succeeding, both inside and outside the workplace. Make success your weapon of choice.

- Some people both inside and outside the workplace seethe with hatred over your success. They hate to see your success, they hate to hear about your success, they hate to hear about your family's success, and they hate others to see you as successful. People who know me will hate this book, not only because of the content but also because *I* wrote it and stand to make a nickel from the sales. I can't wait to read the bogus and sabotaging book reviews.

- People label what they don't understand. For example, if you live in an expensive house or drive an expensive car, these people will tell themselves that you're living above your means, because it helps them sleep at night. If you graduate from a college or university that others deem a "big deal", they'll tell themselves it's because of affirmative action, because it helps them sleep at night. If you get a promotion, such people will tell themselves you had an unfair advantage, because it helps them sleep at night. Get it? Marginalizing your accomplishments helps people feel better about their inability to measure up. Notice, they don't marginalize the accomplishments of those who don't share your skin color because success for them is the norm, not the exception.

CHAPTER 16

I'm Done

* * *

Writing this book was a labor of love, with the emphasis on *labor*. The easiest part of the book-writing process was uttering the words "I will write a book." Execution proved to be more difficult and to take much longer than I expected.

During the past eighteen months, I had many sleepless nights in which the only sound piercing the still darkness of the house was the sound of my fingers pounding away at the keyboard to keep up with an overactive brain that recalled experiences along my professional journey in rapid succession. Recalling these experiences also brought forth associated emotions from within that I didn't know were still there. Some nights were more emotionally draining than others, but despite it all, writing during these times was effortless—a writer's dream that I didn't take for granted, because I knew it wouldn't always be that way.

Other times when I sat down to write, my head felt like a big bowl of alphabet-soup with few vowels. Any attempt I made to create a single word would result in frustration and wasted time. No arrangement of letters generated anything usable despite my best efforts.

Just when I thought that writing couldn't become any more challenging, there were times I sat down to write, my brain would become empty. Though my eyes stared at the computer screen and I concentrated intensely, my brain was a black hole, devoid of anything remotely usable. Days turned into weeks of writer's-block nothingness. Alphabet-soup brain didn't seem so bad on those days, because with a brain full of alphabets, I at least had a chance to string letters together to create a word. A brain full of nothing will yield nothing every time.

The most endearing times were when I sat down to write or when I was in the middle of writing and I heard a voice yell, "Da-deeee!" That was all it took for me to redirect 100 percent of my focus to another game of peekaboo or another round of "If you're happy and you know it, clap your hands!"

Because of the challenges and setbacks that I endured over the past 18 months, I now have a heightened level of respect and admiration for authors and writers everywhere. Whether you write books, articles, newsletters, or blogs, my hat's off to you. Writing *this* book was difficult.

I'll close with one of my favorite Bible passages, Psalm 31 (NIV). I sincerely hope that it will provide a measure of comfort for the unique challenges and frustrations you may face along your professional journey in corporate America.

In you, LORD, I have taken refuge;
let me never be put to shame;
deliver me in your righteousness.
Turn your ear to me,
come quickly to my rescue;
be my rock of refuge,
a strong fortress to save me.
Since you are my rock and my fortress,
for the sake of your name lead and guide me.
Keep me free from the trap that is set for me,
for you are my refuge.
Into your hands I commit my spirit;
deliver me, LORD, my faithful God.
I hate those who cling to worthless idols;
as for me, I trust in the LORD.
I will be glad and rejoice in your love,
for you saw my affliction
and knew the anguish of my soul.
You have not given me into the hands of the enemy
but have set my feet in a spacious place.
Be merciful to me, LORD, for I am in distress;

my eyes grow weak with sorrow,
my soul and body with grief.
My life is consumed by anguish
and my years by groaning;
my strength fails because of my affliction,
and my bones grow weak.
Because of all my enemies,
I am the utter contempt of my neighbors
and an object of dread to my closest friends—
those who see me on the street flee from me.
I am forgotten as though I were dead;
I have become like broken pottery.
For I hear many whispering,
"Terror on every side!"
They conspire against me
and plot to take my life.
But I trust in you, Lord;
I say, "You are my God."
My times are in your hands;
deliver me from the hands of my enemies,
from those who pursue me.
Let your face shine on your servant;
save me in your unfailing love.
Let me not be put to shame, Lord,
for I have cried out to you;
but let the wicked be put to shame
and be silent in the realm of the dead.

Let their lying lips be silenced,
for with pride and contempt
they speak arrogantly against the righteous.
How abundant are the good things
that you have stored up for those who fear you,
that you bestow in the sight of all,
on those who take refuge in you.
In the shelter of your presence you hide them
from all human intrigues;
you keep them safe in your dwelling
from accusing tongues.
Praise be to the LORD,
for he showed me the wonders of his love
when I was in a city under siege.
In my alarm I said,
"I am cut off from your sight!"
Yet you heard my cry for mercy
when I called to you for help.
Love the LORD, all his faithful people!
The LORD preserves those who are true to him,
but the proud he pays back in full.
Be strong and take heart,
all you who hope in the LORD.

Made in the
USA
Columbia, SC